Understanding Architectural Drawings and Historical Visual Sources

Understanding Architectural Drawings and Historical Visual Sources

Edited by Susie Barson

 Historic England

Published by Historic England, The Engine House, Fire Fly Avenue, Swindon SN2 2EH
www.HistoricEngland.org.uk

Historic England is a Government service championing England's heritage and giving
expert, constructive advice.

© Historic England 2019

First published 2019

ISBN 978-1-84802-370-3

British Library Cataloguing in Publication data
A CIP catalogue record for this book is available from the British Library.

The right of Elain Harwood, Olivia Horsfall Turner, Ian Leith, Adam Menuge and Gordon
Higgott to be identified as authors of this work has been asserted by them in accordance
with the Copyright, Designs and Patents Act 1988.

For more information about images from the Historic England Archive, contact Archive
Services Team, Historic England, The Engine House, Fire Fly Avenue, Swindon SN2 2EH;
telephone (01793) 414600.

Brought to publication by Sarah Enticknap, Publishing, Historic England.

Typeset in Georgia Pro 9/11pt

Edited by Sara Hulse, Write Communications Ltd
Indexed by Alan Rutter
Page layout by Matthew Wilson

Printed in the UK by Gomer Press

Front cover: (Left) Painting of St Andrew's Church, Wells Street, Marylebone c 1846 by
George Hawkins [© London Metropolitan Archives (City of London)] and (right) photograph
of the same church rebuilt to the original design by Samuel Daukes (1845–47) in Kingsbury
in 1934. [© Historic England Archive DP155327]

Frontispiece: Exterior view of Wells Cathedral surrounded by a dramatic black sky with a
photographer perched on a ladder in the foreground. [© Historic England Archive DP044641]

Contents

Contributors

Susie Barson is a senior architectural investigator with Historic England and manager of Historic Places Investigation Team South.

Dr Elain Harwood is a senior investigator with Historic England specialising in the architecture of the 20th century. She is the author of *Space, Hope, and Brutalism: English Architecture, 1945–1975* (Yale University Press, 2015) and co-editor of the series Twentieth Century Architecture and Twentieth Century Architects published by the Twentieth Century Society and Historic England.

Dr Gordon Higgott was a senior investigator with English Heritage. He is now an independent historian specialising in the study of architectural drawings and design practice in Britain from the 16th to the 18th centuries, with particular emphasis on the work of Inigo Jones and Sir Christopher Wren. He recently published online catalogues of English Baroque drawings at Sir John Soane's Museum and Wren-office drawings at St Paul's Cathedral, and is currently preparing an online catalogue of 18th-century drawings at Westminster Abbey.

Dr Olivia Horsfall Turner is senior curator of designs at the Victoria and Albert Museum where she is responsible for the national collection of design drawings, documenting the creative process in art, architecture and design from the 14th century to the present day. She was formerly an architectural investigator at English Heritage and a historian with the Survey of London. A specialist in British architecture from the 16th to the 18th centuries, she is currently preparing a new catalogue of the drawings of Robert and John Smythson in the RIBA collection.

Ian Leith FSA works in the Historic England Archive handling acquisitions, provenance and documentation. He is one of the founders of the Public Monuments and Sculpture Association (PMSA), which has provided data for the Historic England Programme for Public Art in 2016. He is currently researching the architects and engineers who occupied chambers around the Adelphi in Westminster between the 1830s and 1930s.

Dr Adam Menuge investigated and researched historic buildings and places for the Royal Commission on the Historical Monuments of England and English Heritage between 1990 and 2013, drawing on this experience when teaching professional training courses and producing sector guidance documents on recording buildings and historic area assessment as well as studies of Berwick-upon-Tweed and the Anfield district of Liverpool. He is now course director for the MSt in Building History at the University of Cambridge.

Foreword

The vast array of visual sources that can be drawn on by those researching and investigating historic buildings and areas can be bewildering, even for the most experienced practitioners. In addition to using primary documents and publications and alongside the investigation of the physical fabric, using available visual sources is a crucial part of the process of obtaining a rounded understanding of the historical development of a building and its significance.

This book, written by leading experts in the field, provides a broad overview of available visual sources – in the main, drawings, topographical views, maps, and photographs – where they can be found and how they should be used and interpreted. Along with its companion document *Understanding Historic Buildings: A Guide to Good Recording Practice* (rev edn, 2016), it originally formed part of a programme of English Heritage (now Historic England) guidance on approaches to investigating the built historic environment. It is based on the content of a training course on visual sources developed and delivered by former English Heritage Senior Architectural Investigator Dr Gordon Higgott, with input from Dr Adam Menuge and other colleagues. The book has been expertly edited into a seamless narrative by Susie Barson.

For heritage professionals and architectural historians the book will help them decide what sources are worth checking in the available time and how to use and interpret them. For those researching a building in their city, town or village or as part of a family history project, it will open up a new and exciting world of visual material, which by its very nature renders the physical evidence of the past more tangible. The book also serves as a gateway to relevant published guides and increasing numbers of online resources containing visual material. It is not exhaustive in its coverage but it is the first time such guidance has been brought together in a single volume. We hope it will delight, inspire and illuminate in equal measure.

John Cattell
Head of Investigation & Analysis
Historic England

Acknowledgements

This guidance grew out of a professional training course 'Researching Architectural Drawings and Historic Visual Sources' directed by Dr Gordon Higgott with Adam Menuge on behalf of English Heritage, with topics presented by the authors.

The authors and editors are grateful for the help, knowledge and insights of a number of professional historians and archivists in the preparation of this guidance, and their assistance with image reproduction and granting of copyright permissions. Individuals in Historic England who merit special thanks are John Cattell, Pete Herring, Chris Redgrave, Rebecca Burns, Nigel Wilkins, Ian Savage, Mike Evans, Paul Backhouse and Sarah Enticknap. David Adshead and Neil Burton also provided helpful advice and suggestions.

Introduction

This document is intended as an initial guide for those wishing to find and interpret original architectural drawings, maps, topographical views, photographs and other historic visual sources when researching historic buildings and sites. It describes the common conventions in architectural drawing, print-making, map-making and photography in Britain from the 16th century to the present day, and lists the most widely used archives, online databases and published sources. It explains methods of researching and interpreting primary visual material and points out the insights to be gained and the pitfalls to be avoided. It will be of particular interest to historic buildings professionals, archaeologists, conservation architects, students of architectural history and those involved in the preparation of conservation plans. More widely, it is hoped that the visual sources discussed and listed here may open up a new and rich vein of material to different kinds of historians, genealogists, educators, students and authors.

Original design drawings, record drawings, surveys, maps, topographical views and photographs often provide valuable evidence for understanding historic buildings and sites. Interpreting such material requires knowledge of historic design and mapping conventions, the role of the drawings in the construction process, the methods and techniques used to create engraved or topographical views, and the equipment and processes used in photography at particular times. How do we evaluate fragmentary visual and documentary evidence for lost or altered historic buildings and interiors, and how do we interpret anonymous early architectural plans, sections and elevations?

The 19th and 20th centuries present a vast array of visual sources and documentary material, from tithe and Ordnance Survey maps to local authority building control plans and illustrations in the trade and popular press. From the 19th century, the development of the architectural profession resulted in a wealth of competition drawings, as well as drawings for commercial clients and private individuals, many of which have been deposited in publicly accessible collections such as the Royal Institute of British Architects Drawings Collection, the Victoria and Albert Museum and the National Archives. The popularity of photography in this period has given rise to a number of important photographic collections of buildings such as the Robert Elwall Photographs Collection at the Royal Institute of British Architects and the Historic England Archive. The challenge is finding the material and prioritising avenues of research. Researchers of all periods must be aware of the pitfalls involved in the analysis of original graphic, printed or photographic material, as well as the benefits that can be gained.

Historic visual sources can be found in national, local and private collections. Catalogues of national collections are increasingly available online. Catalogues of archives in local collections are usually listed on the National Archives website: www.nationalarchives.gov.uk. Very often archives will include entire deposits from local country houses and estates. However, original drawings and historic photographs are also often found in the surviving buildings themselves – framed on the walls, or in boxes in a storeroom – and both persistence and diplomacy may be needed to gain access to them. Where important visual sources are held in places other than record offices, archives and other recognised collections that have procedures to ensure security, access and conservation, it is strongly recommended that the owner's permission be sought for making copies, scans or photographs. The resulting reproductions can then be placed with a suitable repository as an insurance against the loss of the originals.

1 | Architectural drawings

When studying historic visual sources, the first question is: What was it for? We need to know what information the image was intended to convey, and to whom. It might have been created to give an overall impression or to specify details – for the architect, a patron, a mason or a visitor. The second question is: What is its stage of realisation? We need to know the relationship between the drawing or representation and the subject depicted. In all periods, design work on paper proceeded through several stages of realisation. The image might be a sketch or preliminary design, a competition design, a finished or presentation design, a contract drawing or a working drawing. All these are part of the evolution of the design before the building is constructed. Alternatively, it might be an image of an extant building, either to provide a record of existing work prior to making alterations or to document a new building after it has been finished.

When researching architectural drawings, it is essential to try to establish at the outset the stage in the design or recording process to which the example belongs, and to be aware of the potential for extracting information from it about actual or intended qualities or features of the completed building. Drawings of unbuilt designs can be extremely interesting, both in their own right and because unrealised schemes may have influenced what was eventually built either on that site or in another context.

Types of architectural drawings

The sketch

Examples of the architectural sketch survive from as early as the 16th century. Architectural sketches assume particular importance where they are the only evidence of the designer's intention before it was handed to an assistant for working up into a more finished form. They may hold vital clues for understanding the purpose and character of the completed building. Sketches are typically freehand, with no scale, but will often contain the essential concepts of the completed scheme or demonstrate the thought process behind a solution for a particular design problem (Fig 1.1).

Fig 1.1
Denys Lasdun's freehand sketch of 1978 for the IBM Building, to the east of the National Theatre in London (1969–77; Grade II*), demonstrates his intention to create a solid visual link with the National Theatre and Waterloo Bridge through the shared horizontal 'strata' of the terraces, which are firmly expressed in the pencil drawing. [© RIBA Collections, DLCT1149]

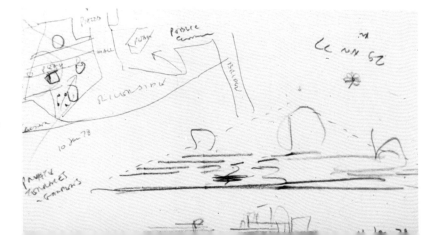

The preliminary design

After the sketch, the more fully drawn out design is often called the preliminary design. It is usually drawn to scale with a ruler, and represents the stage at which a client may ask for revisions. The architect may produce a number of drawings of the same character, or incorporate variants on the same sheet. Such designs can inform the direction the final design will take, and may include details that were executed but have since disappeared from the fabric. In the 17th and early 18th centuries, when paper was relatively expensive, architects often introduced alternatives on the same sheet, either side of the axis of a plan or elevation (Fig 1.2).

The finished design

The finished design is the final, complete scheme, drawn up in a formal set of plans, elevations and possibly sections. The drawings are usually 'finished' with shading or wash and have minimal annotations (Fig 1.3). Finished designs of any period may be modified in execution, but this was especially true before the mid-18th century, at which point architects began routinely to engage assistants to make copies of their designs.

There are virtually no surviving complete finished designs for any major building in Britain from the 16th and 17th centuries, because the originals were passed to the masons' workshops for the preparation of construction or working drawings, and were either lost or destroyed in the process. Thus, when a neatly finished drawing does survive from this period, it probably does not represent the final stage of the design.

Fig 1.2
Sir James Thornhill, preliminary design for a ceiling at an unidentified building, with alternatives on both axes of the plan, 1720s–30s. [© Sir John Soane's Museum, London. Photo: Hugh Kelly (111/55)]

Fig 1.3
William Dickinson, finished design
for Westminster School Dormitory,
1714. [All Souls College, Oxford,
G.380 (III.35), by kind permission
of The Warden and Fellows of All
Souls College, Oxford]

The presentation design

The presentation design is a highly finished drawing made to impress a patron, client or competition judge, as well as to explain the scheme. Such drawings are never annotated with dimensions, but may bear inscriptions. From the late 18th century onwards, the presentation design was usually rendered in perspective, as shown in the perspective by Joseph Michael Gandy (1771–1843) of the breakfast room at Sir John Soane's Pitzhanger Manor in Ealing, c 1802 (Fig 1.4).

Such drawings should not be confused with topographical perspectives of completed buildings or interiors. Gandy's drawing appears to show the completed interior but has been demonstrated to predate construction, as the colour scheme in Soane's design does not correspond with that discovered in paint scrapes of the room itself. Other clues will give away a drawing as a design proposal rather than a record of the completed building, for example, unrealised features in the fabric (discoverable from comparing the drawing with other visual sources) or the method of presentation itself.

Fig 1.4
Joseph Michael Gandy, design perspective for the breakfast room, Pitzhanger Manor, c 1802. Gandy has framed the view with a stage curtain, indicating that the interior on display belongs to the realm of fiction rather than fact. [© Sir John Soane's Museum, London (P95)]

The working drawing

The purpose of the working drawing is to convey practical information to those involved in the construction process. Large-scale working drawings exist from the medieval period in the form of incisions of moulding profiles in stone or plaster, but surviving examples on paper are rare before the late 16th century and until the late 18th century very few complete sets of working drawings survive. By the 1820s architects imposed control on all design and construction details. The process of drawing them was greatly facilitated by the increasing availability of paper of different sizes and qualities from English paper mills.

Colour coding of building materials on drawings – first found on Sir Christopher Wren's (1632–1723) early architectural drawings in the 1660s, and routinely adopted by George Dance the Younger (1741–1825) from the 1780s – became standard in the 19th century and helped to distinguish cast iron, brick, stone, studwork and other structural materials from cladding and surface decoration (Fig 1.5).

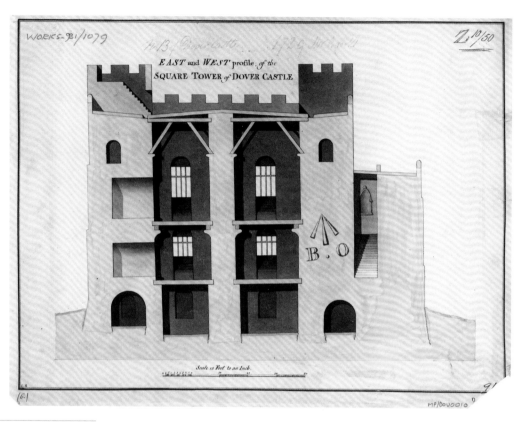

The record drawing

The record drawing is a copy of the architect's design, prepared by the architect
or by a draughtsman. It can easily be confused with a survey drawing of the
built fabric itself. Robert and James Adam (1728–1792; 1732–1794) were
the first architects in private practice known to have engaged draughtsmen
to prepare copies of completed designs, either for the office record, or for
publication in engraved form in their *Works in Architecture* (1773–79). Such
drawings cannot be relied upon as accurate records of the completed fabric,
and researchers should always seek to establish the place of such drawings
in the chronology of design and construction. A case in point is a 'duplicate'
drawing of Robert Adam's ceiling design for the library at Kenwood House in
1767 (Fig 1.6).

Sir John Soane (1753–1837) developed a much more thorough system
of recording his designs than the Adam brothers had ever attempted: office
draughtsmen prepared copies of the design at several stages and Soane often
sent his perspective artist, Joseph Michael Gandy, to draw the completed
building. The result is a deceptively uniform method of rendering buildings
either as designs or completed structures, and care must be taken to verify the
stage of realisation of such drawings.

Another type of record drawing is that produced by antiquaries, architects
and archaeologists, who from the 17th century onwards produced views, plans
and measured surveys of buildings and monuments.

Fig 1.6
Office of Robert and James Adam:
copy of Robert Adam's ceiling
design for Kenwood House, 1767.
Through a paint scrape analysis
of the ceiling in 1969, the strong
pinks and greens in this drawing
were found not to have been
executed, even though Adam had
himself praised these very colours
in his account of the design in
Works in Architecture (1773–79).
[© Sir John Soane's Museum,
London. Photo: Ardon Bar-Hama
(Adam volume 11/113)]

Kenwood.

N Duplicate
1767

The contract drawing

The contract drawing is a final design for execution and formed part of the contract signed by the building contractor, client and architect. Such drawings first appeared in the late 17th century but proliferated from the early 19th century with the emergence of independent building contractors, who submitted tenders for work and required fully annotated plans. In this period working drawings were often signed by contractors as a means of verifying building materials and dimensions before construction (Fig 1.7).

A short history of architectural drawing projections and conventions, c 1530–c 2000

Architectural drawing in the sense of design and record drawing emerged in Britain as a separate genre in the early 16th century with the wider availability of drawing paper, made from rags and linen. Vellum, made from calf skin, was used from the medieval period until the early 17th century. It offered a superior drawing surface for precise records and surveys but was far more expensive than paper. From the mid-16th century it became the support medium for prestige drawings rather than working designs.

Fig 1.7

Francis Edwards, working and contract drawing for the roof structure of St John the Baptist, Hoxton, 1824. This is one of 56 drawings produced by Francis Edwards (1784–1857) for St John the Baptist, covering every detail of the church's design. They helped the Commissioners for the Church Building Act of 1818 ensure that building costs were strictly monitored. [© RIBA Collections, Francis Edwards Vol, Shelf B4]

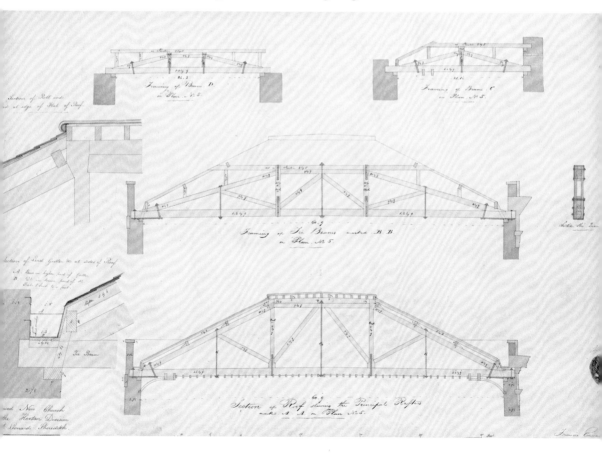

In the 16th century, scaled plans and elevations of buildings (then known respectively as 'platts', 'plots' or 'platforms', and 'uprights' or 'fronts') gradually replaced pictorial views. This was underpinned by surveyors using more sophisticated measuring equipment and calculating distances, heights and orientation with principles of triangulation derived from the classical author Euclid, whose *Geometry* was available in English from 1570. These principles were widely disseminated through surveying manuals like Leonard Digges's popular *A Boke Named Tectonicon*, which ran to 18 issues between 1556 and 1656. Throughout the 16th century and well into the 17th century, architectural elevations continued to display 'pictorial' elements in perspective and such drawings generally cannot be relied upon as scaled records of design proposals or built works.

In the mapping of towns and counties, the chorographic view, in which landscape and buildings are viewed obliquely, pictorially and often out of scale with each other (Fig 1.8), gave way in the 1550s and 1560s to the ichnographic plan (from *ichnos*, the Greek word for track or footprint). This is a scaled representation, drawn by plotting distances with the aid of a compass and measuring rod. In 16th-century examples the radiating lines of the compass dial are usually imposed on the map, along with the scale. The earliest recorded example is a plan of Portsmouth in 1545; a particularly fine example is a manuscript map of Berwick-upon-Tweed prepared by Rowland Johnson in about 1561 (Fig 1.9). Such plans continued to display architectural features in 'laid-flat' elevation, and it was not until the mid-18th century that estate and town plans became entirely rational in their drawing and mapping conventions (Fig 1.10). The decisive influence at this time was John Rocque's mapping of English towns, using a theodolite to take bearings from steeples and measure angles from street corners. Rocque's maps of Bristol (1743), Exeter (1744), Shrewsbury (1746) and his published map of London in 1747 – the *Plan of the Cities of London and Borough of Southwark* on a scale of 200 feet to the inch (1:2400) – set the standard for all future town plans in Britain.

In 16th-century France, Jacques Androuet du Cerceau (1510–1584) had established a style of single-point and two-point perspective drawing in elaborative views of chateaux in his *Les plus excellents bastiments de France* (1576). In the 17th century, French architectural and topographical illustrators – the Marots, the Lepautres and Adam Perelle – developed the bird's-eye perspective by elevating the sight lines. These conventions influenced English draughtsmanship and architectural engraving towards the end of the 17th century, spurred on by the emigration to Britain of Huguenot illustrators from France and the Low Countries, including Daniel Marot (1661–1752), Jan Kip (1653–1722) and Leonard Knyff (1650–1721) (Fig 1.11).

In the 17th century, architects, masons and others who prepared architectural drawings in Britain began using orthogonal drawing conventions. 'Orthogonal' means 'involving right angles'. It is a method of drawing every part of a design to scale, in plan, section and elevation, without perspective, so that depth of recession can be measured by seeing the plan in relation to the elevation. The plan and section are cuts through a building, the plan being a horizontal cut and the section being a vertical cut, while the elevation is a frontal view made in projection on a vertical plane. Thus, each can be related to the other by reference to a common scale. Inigo Jones (1573–1652) introduced these conventions into British architectural drawing practice after touring Italy in 1613–1614 and studying buildings by Andrea Palladio (1508–1580) alongside illustrations in his treatise *I Quattro Libri dell'Architettura* (1570),

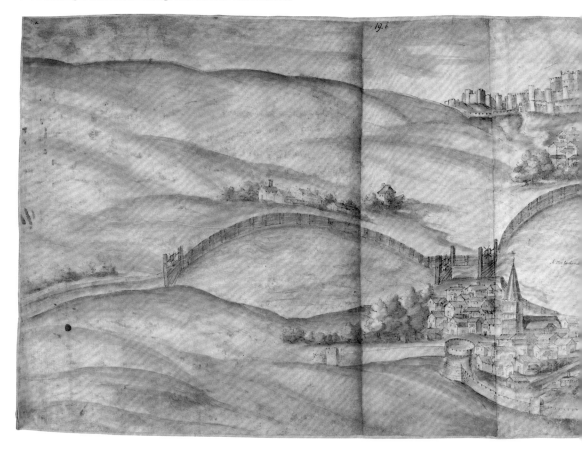

Fig 1.8
Chorographic view of a
proposed new harbour at
Dover by Vincenzo Volpe, 1532.
[© British Library, Cotton
Augustus I. i. 19 BL008776]

Fig 1.9
Ichnographic map of Berwick-
upon-Tweed, prepared by
Rowland Johnson in about 1561.
[Hatfield House, Maps CPM I.22]

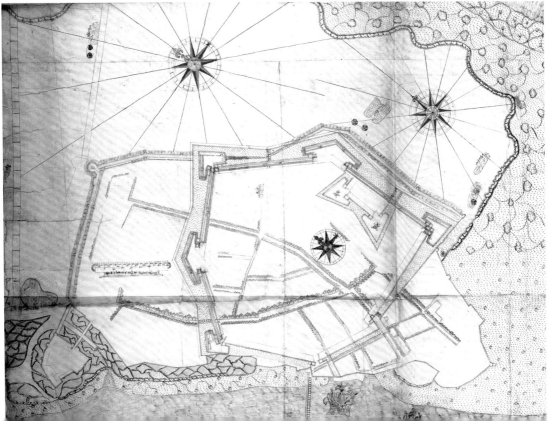

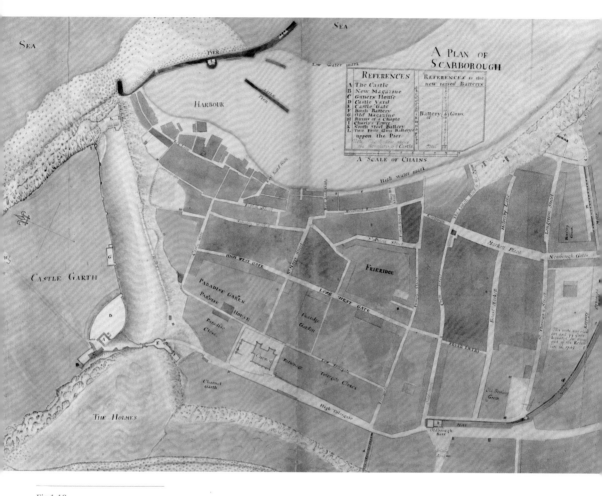

Fig 1.10
This map of Scarborough from the late 1740s illustrates the emergence of fully scaled mapping conventions for town plans in the mid-18th century. The unknown cartographer was probably connected with the Office of the Ordnance, as the map illustrates fortifications put in place after the Jacobite Rebellion in 1745. [© Sir John Soane's Museum, London. Photo: Hugh Kelly (111/44)]

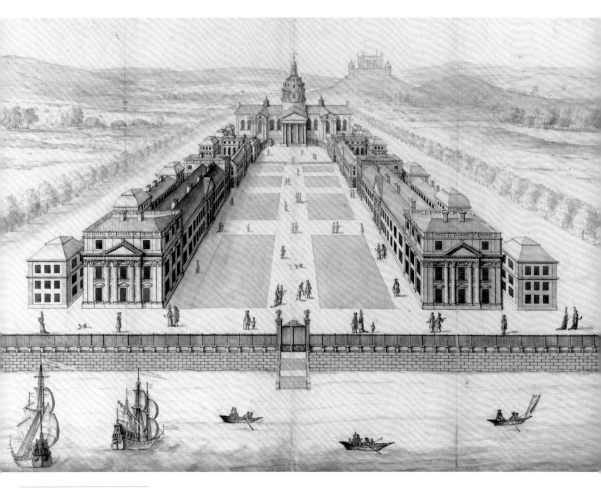

Fig 1.11
Bird's-eye views, such as this
depiction of Greenwich Hospital
by Leonard Knyff, c 1695, were
pioneered in Britain by émigré
illustrators. [© Sir John Soane's
Museum, London. Photo: Hugh
Kelly (111/4)]

in which he used orthogonal methods of representation throughout. By the late 17th century these conventions were standard in design work prepared under the direction of Sir Christopher Wren in the Royal Works, St Paul's Cathedral and the office responsible for rebuilding the City churches (Fig 1.12).

From the second decade of the 18th century, architectural publication began to determine and dominate English architectural drawing practice. Lord Burlington (1694–1753) and his draughtsmen Henry Flitcroft (1697–1769), Colen Campbell (1676–1729), James Gibbs (1682–1754), Isaac Ware (1704–1766) and John Vardy (1718–1765) all prepared design drawings for publication using a grey-wash technique intended as a guide to the engraver and derived from French design practice in the late 17th century (*see* Fig 1.3). Finished drawings in the 1720s and 1730s are extremely difficult to attribute. In terms of technique, the quill pen gave way to the fine brass ruled pen, and draughtsmen learned to apply wash with perfect smoothness.

By the mid-18th century, large well-established offices had easily recognisable 'house styles', which included scales, notation of dimensions, borders and, above all, lettering. Examining these features can help to identify the originating office of a drawing. Finished drawings from the Office of Works (responsible for Crown and government buildings) are usually in a smoothly graduated grey-wash shading technique. Coloured washes on drawings are often highly significant of authorship and can only be appreciated by studying the originals. James Gibbs used a delicate grey, Robert Adam a much darker one, Sir John Soane a yellowish-brown.

In contrast to the grey-wash conventions used by architects and draughtsmen in the Office of Works, those in the Office of the Royal Ordnance (responsible for military buildings) continued to use coloured washes and a range of pictorial conventions. They were influenced in part by architectural drawing practice in the Dutch Republic in the mid-17th century, where building materials were differentiated by colour. These drawing conventions were transmitted to England by the Dutch-born engineer Bernard de Gomme (1620–1685), who became Surveyor General of the Ordnance in 1682. In Board of Ordnance drawings masonry is usually shaded in red (whether it is of stone or brick), timber in brown, and lead roofs in blue (*see* Fig 1.5).

The perspective views of Kip and Knyff's three-volume *Nouveau Théâtre de la Grande Bretagne* (1700) had a powerful effect on architectural draughtsmanship in Britain. As well as this inspiration, illustrators were given the techniques they needed to accomplish accurate (or seemingly accurate) perspective renderings of buildings by an English translation of Andrea Pozzo's *Perspectiva Pictorum et Architectorum* of 1693, which was published in 1707 with the 'approbation' of Sir Christopher Wren. However, although English textbooks on perspective became plentiful from the second decade of the 18th century, it was not until the 1770s that British architects made regular use of perspective conventions in design drawings. An early manifestation was the watercolour perspective of a design set in a pictorial landscape. It was used by Robert Adam (1728–1792) and Sir William Chambers (1723–1796), both of whom had been influenced by Charles-Louis Clérisseau (1721–1820) and Giovanni Battista Piranesi (1720–1778) in Paris and at the French Academy in Rome. The foundation of the Royal Academy at old Somerset House in London in 1768 proved a great stimulus for the development of the 'design' perspective, as many such renderings were prepared for exhibition alongside oil and watercolour paintings.

Fig 1.12
Wren office, St Paul's Cathedral,
upper transept front, c 1685–
1686, in elevation, section and
plan, and with internal elevation
of the upper window, drawn using
orthogonal drawing conventions.
[© London Metropolitan Archives
(City of London), St Paul's
Collection, WRE/3/2/5 (D.46), by
kind permission of The Chapter of
St Paul's Cathedral]

Topographical drawing originated in the 17th-century study of county history. Antiquaries and archaeologists produced drawings intended to document sites that were threatened by decay or destruction. Images also facilitated comparison of buildings for study. These records were sometimes published in county histories, in antiquarian surveys, or in publications such as the *Gentleman's Magazine* (from 1731), but many more remain in manuscripts in record offices, libraries and museums.

Great advances were made in the accurate rendering of townscapes and buildings from the 1740s onwards through the use of the camera obscura, an optical device that projects the image of its surroundings onto a screen. A leading exponent of this technique was Thomas Sandby (1721–1798), who became the first Professor of Architecture at the Royal Academy of Arts and who with his brother Paul (1731–1809) established a genre of topographical and perspective drawing of almost photographic accuracy (Fig 1.13).

Fig 1.13
Detail from Thomas Sandby, Windsor from the Goswells drawn in a Camera, c 1760s. [RCIN 914602, Royal Collection Trust/© Her Majesty Queen Elizabeth II 2018]

Competition drawings

In the 19th century, a dramatic increase in the number of building projects and the expansion of the architectural profession meant that architects and designs were often chosen by competition. Competitions were most often held for national or civic schemes, and drawings were produced for a wide variety of buildings, including town halls, libraries, hospitals, churches and memorials. Architectural competitions were not a 19th-century innovation – the Mansion House in London, for example, was the outcome of a competition in 1737 – but during that period they became the prevalent method of determining a design, although they were often criticised for unfairness. Winners usually, though not always, received a premium for their designs, but were not necessarily appointed as the builders of their scheme. Advertisements for competitions and the details of any conditions were published in the national press, inviting entries in the form of drawings and models and often attracting large numbers of applicants. The 1834 competition for the Houses of Parliament prompted almost 100 schemes comprising nearly 1,000 drawings, but even less prestigious competitions generated numerous entries from architects trying to make their name. As a consequence, there is a large corpus of competition drawings, many of which necessarily represent buildings that were never constructed (Fig 1.14).

Early in the 19th century competition designs were typically colour perspectives, but these were widely criticised as misleading because they included extraneous detail and visual effects as well as architectural information. In the latter part of the century, therefore, pen-and-ink drawings were often specified as the required mode of representation. As competitions were anonymous, drawings were unsigned and instead sometimes carry a pseudonym or cipher, although they may have been annotated later with the architect's name. As well as

Fig 1.14 (opposite)
This design of 1834 by Rickman and Hussey proposed a high Gothic style for the projected Fitzwilliam Museum in Cambridge. The competition was won by George Basevi with a building in the classical idiom. [© RIBA Collections, SB30/2(7)]

each drawing containing information in its own right, comparison of alternative designs can elucidate the context of the ultimate choice. The relationship between the competition drawing and the eventual building is often complex. In some cases, no design was chosen; in others, even a winning design was not necessarily built; in yet others, elements from all the designs might be cherry-picked and amalgamated into an entirely new one. Furthermore, winning designs were also subject to change during the construction process. Details of architectural competitions and comments on individual entries were published in the architectural press (*see* pp 26–29). These can be useful for shedding light on the circumstances of a competition and also provide an insight into contemporary perceptions of style and design. An index exists for all 2,542 competitions recorded in *The Builder* from its inception to the end of the century: Roger H Harper, *Victorian Architectural Competitions: An Index to British and Irish Architectural Competitions in The Builder, 1843–1900*.

The trade and popular press

Particularly for commercial and industrial buildings and sites it is worth exploring the range of trade publications which proliferated from the late 19th century. These include specialist journals and the series of directories arranged not geographically but by trade (by Kelly for a number of trades, and by Worrall for textiles, for example). Journals frequently ran illustrated articles on notable new buildings and on wider trends within a particular industry, and both journals and directories may include advertisements incorporating views of premises or processes (*see* Fig 1.15). For journals, see especially the collections of the British Newspaper Archive. The popular press, which includes a great variety of magazines and miscellanies on topics such as bandstands and breweries, is a less predictable source for images but increasing digitisation and facilities for word searching on the internet make this source increasingly accessible.

Promotional images

Tradesmen and manufacturers were quick to see the importance of views depicting their business premises, initially as a way of ensuring that potential customers found them, and later as a way of projecting an image of the business, for example its scale, solidity and modernity (Fig 1.15). Early images of this kind can be found on 18th-century trade cards, and from the 19th century they become increasingly common as embellishments to letterheads and other printed ephemera. Many are found in the advertisement sections of trade directories and some other publications. By their nature such views may have remained in use for a period of years, and the date found on a surviving letter or invoice may be no better than a *terminus ante quem*. Their accuracy may also be questionable. Promotional images often exaggerated the scale of an enterprise (adding extra storeys or bays to a building, for example), or presented it in a more favourable manner than is warranted by the facts.

Building control records

The regulation of building activity has a continuous history stretching back to the medieval period, at least in England's larger towns. Building control records (also known as building deposit plans) represent an intensification of the process of regulation towards better hygiene through drains and sewers, and good building practice such as to prevent fires. The Public Health Act of 1858 allowed

Fig 1.15 (opposite)
By the early 19th century larger industrial and commercial enterprises saw the value of promoting their business through an image of the firm's premises. This characteristic aerial perspective comes from an advertisement in the Post Office Directory of Yorkshire (London, 1857). [Sheffield Libraries and Archive]

94

Prize Medal, 1851,

AWARDED TO

MARSDEN, BROTHERS, & CO.,

FOR MECHANICS' TOOLS.

BRIDGE STREET WORKS, SHEFFIELD.

MARSDEN, BROTHERS, & CO.,

(LATE FENTON & MARSDEN,)

MANUFACTURERS OF

EDGE AND JOINERS' TOOLS, BRACES AND BITS, AUGERS, SCREW BOXES,

Saws, Files; Pen, Pocket, and Table Cutlery, &c., of superior quality.

STEEL CONVERTERS, REFINERS, AND GENERAL MERCHANTS.

Skate Manufacturers by Special Appointment to The Queen and Royal Family.

local authorities to demand plans of new buildings or alterations; this position was consolidated by a further Act of 1875.

A few authorities have plans from before this date but they tend to be very simple. In London, plans submitted to the Metropolitan Commission of Sewers survive from 1848. The earliest show little more than the location of the main drain, but may help establish a date, client and/or function for the original building; subsequent plans are more detailed and from *c* 1900 onwards full sets of plans and elevations tended to be lodged whether the application was for drains, building licences or even a liquor licence. Plans were also submitted for buildings that broke the conventions of the London Building Acts (legislation that originated with the Great Fire of London, although most surviving plans and related files date from the 20th century). In London, if a building is large, tall, built of unorthodox materials such as concrete or steps forward of the building line, there is a chance that there will be plans for it in the London Metropolitan Archives (LMA) (Fig 1.16). Individual London boroughs have varying survivals of plans, many on microfilm, though some authorities restrict access to owners and their representatives.

Similarly, there is a mixed survival rate among the largest provincial cities: Liverpool introduced legislation as early as 1840 and outer areas may have plans from 1854, but for the city centre plans only survive from 1912 to 1918. While surviving collections of 19th-century plans tend to be in the main cities, from the very end of the century small towns and rural areas were established as local authorities with their own controls that required plans to be submitted. In most places holdings are generally best for the inter-war years (better than for the post-war period), although they can be extremely fragmentary in rural areas. In Dorset, for example, plans survive from 1870 for Bournemouth and from 1880 for Dorchester, but for rural district councils there is nothing before the 1920s and in some areas nothing before the 1950s. Similar drawings are still required for Building Regulations approval, listed building consent and other planning permissions.

Licensing authorities may have plans of pubs, theatres and cinemas. Brewster Sessions plans, collected for the licensing magistrates, can be a helpful backup to records in the planning system. Theatre legislation, controlling not only exits but also sites, seating and circulation areas of all public halls as a means of limiting the spread of fire, originated in 1878; similar legislation to control cinemas – where the risk of fire was even greater because of nitrate film – came into force in January 1910 (Fig 1.17).

Where drawings do not survive, some details may nevertheless be recoverable if the register in which they were noted down on receipt has survived. These registers vary in format from place to place but generally record such details as the building's address, the type of building proposed, and the name of the owner and/or the builder or architect submitting the drawings. Indexing varies from place to place. Relatively few registers have been digitised, and because the registers were compiled in order of submission it can be a time-consuming process to locate records of a particular building, or all the buildings in a street, if their likely date is not already known.

Building control drawings could be submitted by architects, builders, surveyors, owners and agents depending on the scale and prestige of the building. They typically consist of a full set of floor plans and elevations, together with representative cross-sections, and a block plan setting the site in

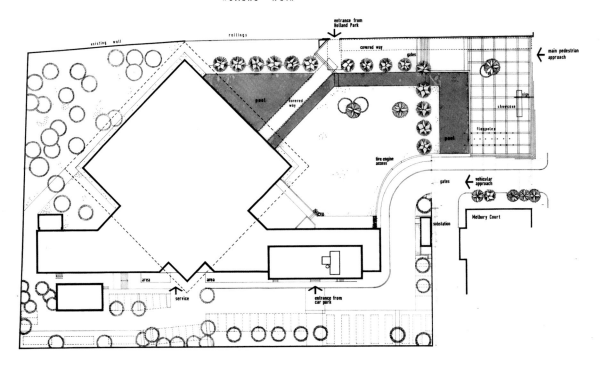

Holland Walk

entrance from
Holland Park

railings

existing wall

covered way

gates

← main pedestrian
approach

pool

covered
way

size

showcase

flagpoles

pool

fire engine
access

gates

← vehicular
approach

substation

Melbury Court

area

area

service

entrance from
car park

Phillimore Gardens

Abingdon Road

Kensington High Street

Holland Walk

Earl's Court Road

Holland Park

SITE FOR
COMMONWEALTH
INSTITUTE

Edwardes Square

Fig 1.16
Robert Matthew, Johnson
Marshall and Partners, plan of the
Commonwealth Institute and Grounds
(February 1959). A series of drawings
of the Commonwealth Institute and its
landscape, unexpectedly found in the
Theatre Plans section of the London
County Council's records, helped in
the redevelopment of the site. [©
London Metropolitan Archives (City of
London), GLC/AR/BR/07/4884]

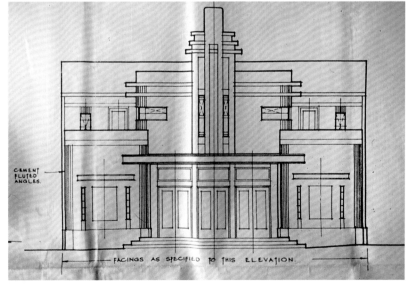

Fig 1.17
The Ritz Cinema, Clipstone,
Nottinghamshire, now
demolished. The pictures show
the building as it was in 2008,
and as designed in 1936 by
Bocock and Kirk. [From Cinema
Licensing Plans at Nottinghamshire
Archives, CC/CL/2/5/2/91]

context (Fig 1.18). The drawings were utilitarian productions in the sense that they were undertaken to secure approval, not to impress clients or professional peers, and some – particularly those prepared by small-scale builders and owners – are rough and ready. They were drawn on a variety of materials – coarse paper, tracing paper and card are all commonly encountered – and therefore have particular conservation problems which may result in illegibility or loss at folds. Most historic building control records are now held by record offices and municipal archives, but some continue to be kept by local planning authorities. A few have been microfilmed.

Once they had been registered, drawings were examined for compliance with the regulations currently in force and either approved or rejected, and the register entry was endorsed accordingly (rejected plans could of course be resubmitted with amendments). Once approved, the plans could be acted upon, but the existence of an approved scheme does not guarantee that the building was ever built, or that it conformed in every respect to the deposited plans. Sometimes new designs were submitted even though a previous set of drawings had been approved. Wherever possible, therefore, the drawings should be checked against the surviving building or other evidence for its existence and form.

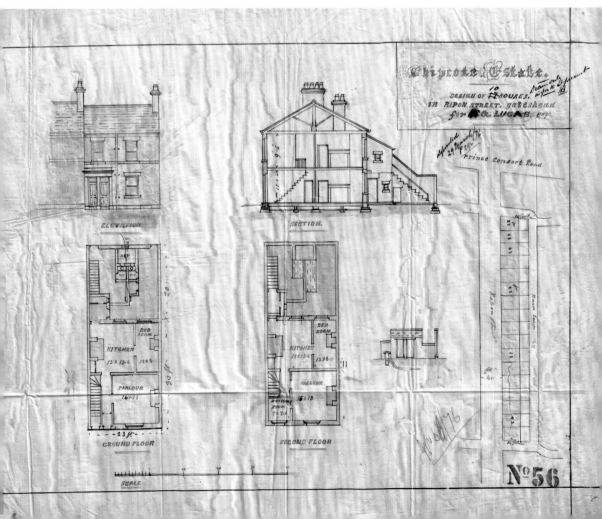

Fig 1.18
Tyneside flats in Ripon St, Gateshead, dated 1876 (unsigned, for the Shipcote Estate). This set of drawings is typical of thousands of building control plans required by local authorities. Tyneside flats superficially resemble conventional terraced houses but each unit consists of two flats, each occupying one floor and having its own front and rear entrance. [Tyne and Wear Archives T311/56/1876]

The architectural periodical press

The emergence of a specialist architectural press is generally dated to 1843, when *The Builder* first appeared. There are some antecedents, such as J C Loudon's *Architectural Magazine*, which enjoyed a brief run from 1834 to 1838. Prior to that, the architectural periodical press, if it can be said to have existed at all, was confined to the more or less regular appearance of architectural or antiquarian articles in journals of a more general character, such as the *Gentleman's Magazine* (from 1731).

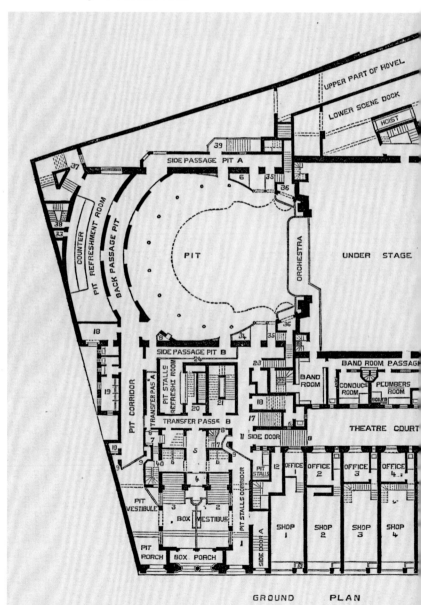

Fig 1.19

Major public and private building projects were published in *The Builder* from 1843 onwards. These plans are for George Corson's design of the Grand Theatre, Leeds. Although lacking the colour and detail of larger architects' drawings these, being tailored to publication, make highly legible illustrations in books and research reports. [© Historic England Archive from *The Builder*, 36 (Nov 16, 1878), 1203]

THE LE

From the advent of *The Builder*, many designs for buildings were published in magazines, with an appraisal, plans and photographs (Fig 1.19). It must be remembered, however, that the original drawings offer more detail, and colour, and can be a valuable tool for seeing how an idea emerged. It should also be noted that publications favoured prestige projects and were prey to factionalism, so the work of some architects and styles was represented more generously than that of others. They are therefore not an unbiased account of the overall output of the architectural profession in a given period.

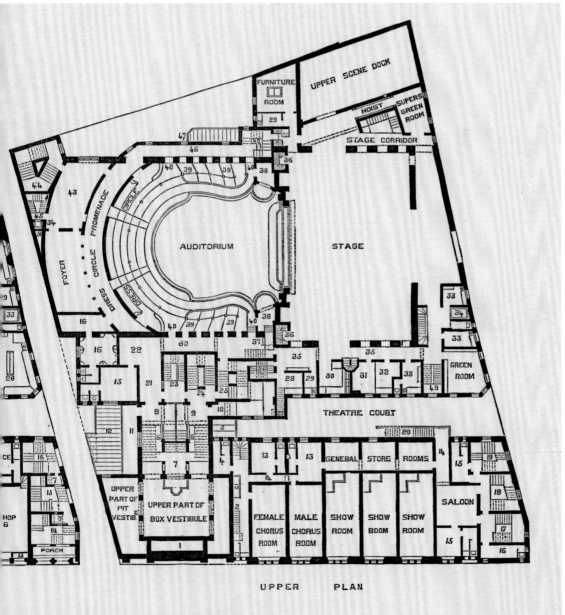

HEATRE AND OPERA HOUSE.——*Plans.*

The Builder (1843) and *Building News* (1855) were joined in the 1890s by a spate of weekly and monthly publications as the invention of the half-tone block in the late 1880s made it possible to publish photographs and type on the same page. These included the *Builders' Journal* in 1895, which has been published as the *Architects' Journal* since 1919; the *Architectural Review* monthly from 1896, and *Architectural Design* in 1930 (originally as *Architectural Design and Construction*, until 1947). The publication of architectural journals followed a similar pattern in other countries, for example in the USA with *Architectural Record* from 1891 and Gustav Stickley's *Craftsman* magazine of 1901, which had an international influence on domestic architecture. More populist magazines also catered to the growing fascination with other people's houses, notably *Country Life* from 1897 and *Ideal Home* from 1911, joined in 1947 by *House and Garden*. These titles can provide details and images lacking in many purely architectural journals.

Younger professions also developed specialist journals, for example *Garden Cities and Town Planning* (now *Town and Country Planning*) was launched as early as 1901, followed by the *Town Planning Review* in 1910. Materials generated their own literature, notably concrete with *Concrete and Concrete Engineering*, begun in 1906, and *Concrete Quarterly* in 1947; steel has a smaller bibliography, although *Building with Steel* (1969–1984) and the international *Acier=Stahl=Steel* are useful. For a time there were a few specialist journals that concentrated on publishing exhibition drawings, of which *Academy Architecture* (1889–1931) is the most important, while the *Liverpool Architectural Sketchbook* from 1910 onwards is a source of student drawings at the key school of the time.

Of still greater significance is the rush of new titles that appeared in the 1920s, which reflected developments in architectural photography, with new viewpoints and bolder images as cameras became more portable and lighting techniques more sophisticated. As H S Goodhart-Rendel said in 1951, 'it is the business of architectural draughtsmanship to convey the design and to record the condition of buildings already existing ... nowadays a large part of this work has been taken away from draughtsmanship by photography' (*RIBA Journal*, Third Series, **58** (4), February 1951, p 127). Particularly useful for buildings of mid-century are the monthly *Building*, founded in 1926 (*Architecture and Building* from 1954 to its demise in 1960), *Architecture Illustrated* from 1930 to 1957 and for cinemas the *Ideal Kinema* (1933–1939). More recent buildings are served by a wealth of commercial and institutional publications, including *Building Design*, founded in 1970, *A3 Times* (1984–1989) and *Architecture Today* (from 1989). The publications of the Architectural Association – *AA Journal*, *AAQ* and (since 1981) *AA Files* – give an insight into the preoccupations of the leading school of architecture in London. As architecture and journalism grew, more international articles on British buildings began to appear in a variety of languages; *Architecture d'Aujourd'hui*, founded in 1931, is helpful on Brutalist architecture, but the dominant European publications are Italian – *Casabella*, *Domus* (both 1928–), *L'Architettura, Cronache e Storia* (1955–) and *Abitare* (1973–), joined since the 1970s by more journals from Germany and Spain, and from Japan with *A+U* (1971–, with little translated into English but many published plans) and its many related monographs and studies.

Runs of the main journals are held by major research libraries, the Royal Institute of British Architects (RIBA) and Historic England Archive, and some large public libraries and university libraries. The first 10 years of *The Builder* is available online and there is a published index to illustrations published in the journal in its first 40 years (Ruth Richardson and Robert Thorne, *The Builder Illustrations Index 1843–1883*, London: The Builder Group & Hutton+Rostron in association with the Institute of Historical Research, 1994). The Avery Index of Periodicals, in published form and online, is a valuable resource. However, for British architecture the starting point is always to look up www.architecture.com, although since it is only 95 per cent complete for buildings before 1972 it is worth checking the handwritten indexes or 'grey books' in the RIBA Library.

From the second quarter of the 19th century antiquarian and archaeological societies, or 'field clubs', proliferated, most covering a single county or a major town and its environs. The journals of these societies, usually well indexed, are a rich source of visual material, generally accompanied by written analysis. The *Victoria County History*, inaugurated in 1897, may be seen as the natural extension of these activities, drawing together scattered knowledge and adding the fruits of systematic research through a range of sources.

Architectural drawings of the 20th century

For 20th-century buildings, drawings are no longer the pre-eminent source of information about an architect-designed development, but just one of a wide range of resources that may include office files, clients' records and third-party sources such as contemporary publications. For the large number of buildings erected by institutions and the public sector there are also records such as minute books. Drawings from this century fall into three main categories: detailed sets of drawings in public collections; architect's design studies and presentation drawings; and concept drawings for schemes never intended to be built.

Detailed design and working drawings held in public collections
Copies of architects' drawings produced to secure planning permission may survive in local authority archives, usually submitted as part of a building control or drainage application, as in the 19th century (*see* pp 20–25) but generally in far greater detail with complete sets of plans. These are helpful both for new buildings and for subsequent alterations to older structures, where the new work is generally outlined in dark pink.

Collections of architects' drawings
The RIBA holds the collections of many of the most distinguished British architects, and its 20th-century holdings are constantly growing. A number of important 20th-century architects' collections are also held by the Historic England Archive, universities and a growing number by county archives. Even where early and unrealised drawings were published, much can be learned from seeing the originals, with their greater detail and use of colour.

As the century progressed, more architects resorted to models, increasingly preferred by committees and clients for their legibility and greater honesty. Indeed, some architects, notably Denys Lasdun (1914–2001), would produce rough sketches and then develop detailed ideas through three-dimensional models rather than drawings – often awkward for historians since they pose greater problems of conservation and storage, and are rarely dated. Other models were produced for exhibition purposes, as when Frederick Gibberd produced models of the future Harlow to impress local residents whose livelihoods were being disrupted by the new town (Fig 1.20). For the more detailed history of architectural models, *see* Chapter 4.

Throughout the 19th and early 20th centuries the architect's preferred medium for communicating the final design for a building, whether for client approval, publication or competition submission, was the drawn or printed perspective. This led to a proliferation of perspective drawing, with the production of presentation works for exhibition and publication that stand as works of art in their own right. Perspectives could show a client or committee

Fig 1.20
A model of the proposed town centre at Harlow by Frederick Gibberd and Partners. As with many models, this one is undated. [By kind permission of the Gibberd Garden Archive, Harlow/© Historic England Archive DP178778]

unaccustomed to reading plans and elevations what a completed building would look like, and they were often highly seductive (Fig 1.21).

A handful of architects became specialised perspectivists and thereafter designed little themselves, notably William Walcot (1874–1943) and Cyril Farey (1888–1954), later joined by R Myerscough Walker (1908–1984), Henry L Gordon Pilkington (1886–1968), John Dean Monroe Harvey (1895–1978) and A C Webb (1888–1975). Of those architects who produced their own perspectives, Robert Atkinson (1883–1952) created a particularly luscious effect with thick colour, and Walcot's perspectives are rich and textured. More common by the middle of the 20th century was the use of delicate watercolours. A finished perspective can be beautiful, but it often tells us little more about a design, unless it differs from the building as completed (Fig 1.22), or represents buildings that were never built. Increasingly, modernists preferred the quick, expressive sketch or a model to convey their intentions to clients, following the example of internationally admired architects such as Erich Mendelsohn, who worked briefly in England in 1933–6.

Fig 1.21

A perspective by Kenneth Browne to illustrate Chamberlin, Powell and Bon's proposals for the Barbican development in the City of London, as revised in 1959. CPB were among the first architects to publish their proposals for a major development in book form. [By kind permission of Frank Woods/© Historic England Archive DP136778, Chamberlin, Powell and Bon archive]

By 1940 perspectives were forbidden as entries in official RIBA competitions, and had to be drawn up hastily for publication when the winner was declared. Consequently, later perspectives lack the richness of earlier examples, and their importance declined save in the hands of specialists such as Sir Basil Spence, for whom they played an important role in promoting his practice. Many perspectives were black and white, to aid their publication, and illustrators used by the *Architectural Review*, notably Gordon Cullen (1914–1994) and Kenneth Browne (1917–2009), received many commissions from other architects.

Cullen and Browne were typical of the post-war era in drawing schemes for publication. They shared a distinctive style with a flair for simplification and a slightly naive Englishness (Fig 1.23). Both architects made extensive use of felt-tip pens, which were first developed in the early 1950s, and of

Fig 1.22

Perspective of Basil Spence's proposed Kensington Town Hall, showing an additional floor, omitted when the design was modified in 1968 to incorporate open-plan offices which required greater floor heights. [© Royal Borough of Kensington and Chelsea Libraries]

Fig 1.23

By the 1950s drawings, photographs and collage were being used to convey ideas as well as information. Gordon Cullen's collage for the *Architectural Review*'s cover in July 1956 questioned the inevitable clash of east and west inherent in Le Corbusier's Law Courts at Chandigarh. [By kind permission of the *Architectural Review*]

collage techniques. Other new aids to drawing were Letraset typefaces, which began as transfers (which tend to fall off over time) and later became wax-adhesive stencils, and Zip-a-Tone (also spelt zipatone), used for lines and especially shading.

Other architects sought new ways of depicting three dimensions on paper. From the 1930s onwards, modernist architects adopted the more rational, scale-based method of illustrating designs three-dimensionally found in the axonometric projection, in which the building is placed at an angle to the plane – usually 45° – and all the dimensions are to scale but there is no perspective reduction in size with distance. Axonometrics were widely used by the Bauhaus and De Stijl architects in the 1920s, before appearing in Britain around 1930 (Fig 1.24). The axonometric became most fashionable in Britain around 1960, when it was adopted by James Stirling (1924–1992) and James Gowan (1923–2015), Stirling going on to use it extensively in his later works of that decade. In the isometric projection (a subset of axonometric) the axes are tilted, so that the right angles are 120° or 60°.

Computer-aided design (CAD) originated in 1963 in a research project at the Massachusetts Institute of Technology, and it began to be pushed into three dimensions from the mid-1970s. In Britain the first three-dimensional CAD designs appeared in 1977, although it was only with advances in programming and high-performance computers in the mid-1980s that the process superseded drawing by hand. It has not only simplified the transmission of an idea but has had an impact on the three-dimensional quality of the designs themselves, well seen in the work of the deconstructivists, and has aided architects and engineers in their realisation.

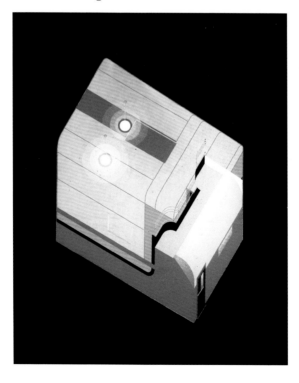

Fig 1.24
An axonometric by Raymond McGrath for the Dance Music and Chamber Music Studio at Broadcasting House, 1929 – a way of reducing a three-dimensional form to a flat image that was more widely adopted after the Second World War. [© RIBA Collections, PA424/4(17)]

Conceptual drawings

Of particular importance from the late 1950s onwards are drawings that are merely conceptual, for schemes there was no intention of building. In the designs of Cedric Price (1934–2003), concepts took the place of real buildings almost entirely, while the members of the Archigram group worked as artists, exhibition designers and theorists more often than as architects. As these architects supported themselves by teaching, their concepts, such as the idea of the 'Walking City', were doubly influential and their drawings are still widely published and exhibited today (Fig 1.25).

EACH WALKING UNIT HOUSES NOT ONLY A KEY ELEMENT OF THE CAPITAL , BUT ALSO A LARGE POPULATION OF WORLD TRAVELLER-WORKERS.

A WALKING CITY

Modern record drawings

Drawings of existing buildings have their roots in the antiquarian tradition of documenting buildings that were threatened by damage or destruction, or that were of special value to scholarship. Many such drawings were – and continue to be – made by architects and their appointed surveyors. During the 20th century, however, with the creation of the royal commissions for England, Scotland and Wales in 1908 and the emergence of local and regional archaeological units and trusts from the 1960s, architects and surveyors were joined by other professionals, although amateur initiatives (notably groups dedicated to documenting vernacular buildings and industrial archaeology) continue to play an important part. Records of the Royal Commission on the Historical Monuments of England (RCHME) are held at the Historic England Archive, together with the records of what was English Heritage. At a local level, Historic Environment Records (HERs) maintained by local authorities are increasingly used as repositories for new records, but others may be found in museums and in the archives of local building recording groups.

As with all record sources, it is important to understand the purpose and circumstances lying behind the creation of historic building records. All records are selective to some degree but the criteria for selection are often not made explicit. Many historic building records omit information relating to modern fabric, and some present only the fabric judged to be 'original' or 'historic', in order that it emerges more clearly in the finished drawing. In many cases the interpretation on which these exclusions have been based may be sound, but may not always be so, and one person's view of what is 'historic' may not be another's.

A further influence on the form, scope and accuracy of a record drawing is the survey method adopted. This is often specified in accompanying documentation, such as a report. Traditional survey methods (sometimes referred to as 'direct survey') employing tapes and rods are capable of producing accurate results in all but the most challenging circumstances, but other survey methods are less dependable, and allowance may be called for when extracting metric or angular information from them. Total station surveys, using an electronic distance measurement (EDM) theodolite, were made from the 1980s onwards. The use of total station equipment may be apparent from the inclusion in the drawing of theodolite 'stations' or, in cruder presentations, of metadata such as 'point numbers' distinguishing individual theodolite observations. The technology is capable of a very high degree of precision, and in practice most such surveys can be relied upon for the extraction of metric and angular data derived directly from the use of the theodolite. However, most total station surveys incorporate varying amounts of direct survey, typically in interiors or other congested or 'blind' areas, so the technical expectations of total station surveys may not be applicable throughout the drawing. Beyond this, there is no simple relationship between the precision of the instrument and the quality of the interpretative data recorded – fragmentary or inconspicuous features and phasing evidence may be under-recorded even when the overall metric accuracy of the survey is high.

The traditional drawing medium for record drawings was pencil or ink, sometimes supplemented by coloured washes, on linen, paper or tracing paper (latterly polyester drafting film). Drawings are usually signed, but the nature of hand drawing means that each draughtsman or woman has in any case a distinct signature, often apparent in lettering or other relatively free-form elements of the drawing (Fig 1.26). Drawings made in a computer-aided design (CAD) programme, widely used since the 1980s, can usually be recognised by a certain machine-like consistency in line-work and a relative absence of signature elements such as characterise the work of individual draughtsmen or women. These drawings, or plots, may present only a portion of the information recorded in the digital file; certain details may be suppressed either because they are judged unsuitable for the purpose in hand or because they will be illegible at the chosen scale. It is also possible that the CAD file may have been revised after the plot was produced. For a variety of reasons, then, it is worth finding out whether a digital file exists and assessing its contents alongside the printed drawing.

Most record drawings, either consciously or unconsciously, observe a series of drawing conventions, but also resort to idiosyncratic or literal representations in the absence of an accepted convention. Drawing conventions have evolved over time, and minor differences or interpretations can be detected in drawings produced by different organisations and even different individuals, which may allow drawings from the same source or hand to be associated with one another. Many will observe a published set of conventions such as the RIBA convention set or those advocated successively by the RCHME and Historic England for record drawings, as outlined in Historic England's *Understanding Historic Buildings: A Guide to Good Recording Practice* (2006; revised 2016).

Fig 1.26
This detailed line drawing, with coloured wash, of Baguley Hall, Manchester, is one of a series made by the former Department of the Environment after it took the building into guardianship. It shows the spere truss dividing the cross-passage from the hall, which has been tree-ring dated to c 1399. The drawing, dated 1972, assigns key numbers to each timber. It also depicts the consequences of structural movement and timber decay, and was intended as an aid to conservation as well as a record of what survives. [© Historic England Archive MP/BAH0025]

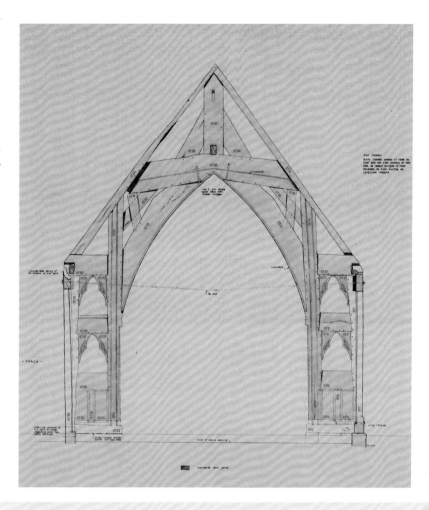

Research questions for architectural drawings

What stage of realisation does the drawing represent? Is it a preliminary design (first ideas); a finished presentation or competition design (before building); a contract drawing or working drawing (for building); a measured or survey drawing, topographical drawing, or a record drawing (after building, or providing a record of an earlier 'design' drawing to a smaller scale)?

What does it show? As well as identifying the building itself and the stage of realisation of the drawing, it is vital to understand what part, level or side of the building is actually shown. First, be sure to identify the aspect of the drawing: is it a plan or part-plan, an elevation, half-elevation, or elevation with alternatives (left and right of central axis), a section, a detail, a perspective, or a bird's-eye view? Plans from the 17th century can display several levels, without indicating a transition from one to the other. Be certain which elevation is shown: the modern-day 'front' of the building may have been the 'back' of the building at an earlier period. In the case of plans, or part-plans, make sure the sheet is correctly orientated (the scale bar will normally be at the bottom of the sheet, although it could be set vertically left or right of the drawing). Refer to other drawings or visual records of the building to check orientation.

When was it made? Accurate dating of the drawing is often crucial for establishing its authorship and purpose. Look first at the style and character of the building represented. Examine the character of the figures or letters on the drawing, and compare with dated examples. A general dating range can be established with reference to surveys of the history of handwriting (eg 'English round hand', c 1690–1730). Where possible, look at the watermark and/or countermark on the sheet. On 'laid paper' (commonly used until the early 19th century), watermarks are translucent marks of manufacture on paper formed by patterns in the mesh of wires used to fix the pulp of rag into a sheet. The name 'laid' derives from the process of laying the pulp on the mesh. The principal mark is normally on one half of the sheet, and a separate shorter cipher or countermark (for example with the initials of the maker) is on the other half. It is often thought that the watermark on the paper is sufficient evidence for dating a drawing. However, from the 16th to the late 18th century, watermarks only provide an approximate date, within a range of 20–40 years (*see* Heawood 1950) (Fig 1.27).

In the second half of the 18th century dating paper by its watermark becomes more precise. English 'Whatman' paper of the 1750s and 1760s is watermarked 'JW', that of the 1770s and 1780s generally 'J Whatman'. An Excise Act in 1794 required that paper made in England should bear a watermarked date. So, from 1794 until 1861, when the Act was repealed, an architectural drawing paper normally bears the date and name of its manufacturer. However, not every paper mill troubled to change the date every year, and nor did every architect necessarily use paper of recent manufacture.

Remember that dates written on drawings need to be interpreted critically. They are not always the date of production of the drawing but could refer to the date when a copy was made as an office record.

Who made it? Every draughtsman has distinct methods of outline, shading, inscription and scale bar conventions. Examples from an unidentified drawing should be compared with securely authenticated examples. A signature on a drawing is not necessarily evidence of the authorship of the drawing itself, nor that the drawing is by a single hand. It may only establish the author of the design. In the 17th century drawings could be prepared by more than one draughtsman, working under the direction of an architect (Fig 1.28).

What is the scale of the drawing? Do not expect the scale to be in neat divisions of an inch or foot. Up to the early 19th century, scales were often arrived at arbitrarily from a subdivision of the width of the sheet of paper, to ensure that the plan or elevation would fit the sheet. The production of larger sheets by Whatman and others from the late 18th century onwards led to the predominance of inch-based scales, unrelated to the size of the sheet. By the mid-19th century the most common scales were 1:48 (¼ inch = 1 ft), 1:96 (⅛ inch = 1 ft) and 1:192 (¹⁄₁₆ inch = 1 ft).

Fig 1.27

An example of a watermark datable within about 40 years is that of the mill of Lubertus van Gerellink (LVG). The pendant LVG beneath a fleur-de-lys is common in the early 18th century. [After Heawood, Watermarks, 1950]

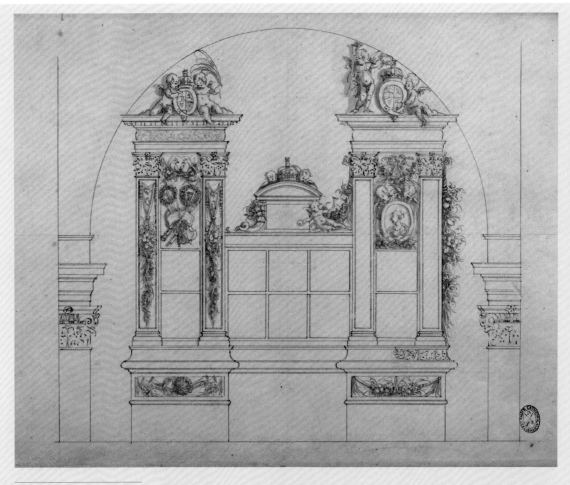

Fig 1.28
Design for the organ case within a choir arch at St Paul's, c 1693, drawn jointly by Nicholas Hawksmoor and Grinling Gibbons. Hawksmoor drew the arcade arch and the frame of the organ case. Within the framework, Gibbons presented alternative decorative schemes to the left and right of the centre line. [© London Metropolitan Archives (City of London), St Paul's Collection, WRE/4/1/1 (D.186), by kind permission of The Chapter of St Paul's Cathedral]

What is its provenance? The provenance of a drawing may provide clues regarding its authorship. Whose collection did it come from? Has it come down to us with drawings by the same architect? A drawing of some age with only a very recent provenance may be of questionable authorship.

What other details offer clues? Pay very careful attention to conventions of line and wash used to mark up plans, sections, elevations, and topographical drawings and maps (eg different types of dotted and dashed lines). These are clues for interpreting what the drawing shows. Remember to record technical information about the drawing – the size of the sheet (height before width, in millimetres), and how it is made up. It may consist of more than one sheet pasted together, and the compilation of the sheet may give clues about the evolution of the design. Note down the inscriptions on the drawing; the simple act of doing this will prompt thought about the purpose of the drawing and ensures an accurate record.

2 | Maps and mapping conventions

Historic maps hold huge potential as evidence for the physical form and date of buildings and associated landscape features. Not all maps will prove equally useful, and while those at quite small scales can undoubtedly provide information, this analysis focuses on maps at scales of 1:10,560 (6 in = 1 mile) and larger. The discussion must begin, however, with an examination of the smaller-scale maps that laid the foundations of English cartography.

County maps and road maps

Maps depicting an entire county (or occasionally two or more counties combined) have existed for all English and Welsh counties since Christopher Saxton's *Atlas of the Counties of England and Wales,* published in 1579 but based on surveys made from the early 1570s onwards. There is good evidence that Saxton's surveys were sponsored by the Crown because of their value for planning national defence at a time of anxiety about foreign attack.

County maps were soon applied to a multitude of uses and were usually intended for publication and sale, sometimes with accompanying letterpress. The scales adopted were sometimes arbitrary in order to fit each map onto a consistent page size, but during the 18th century scales of 2 inches and 1 inch to the mile (1:36,680 and 1:63,360) became increasingly popular. Such maps cannot always be regarded as original surveys. John Speed's county maps, published in his *Theatrum Imperii Magnae Britanniae* (1611) are heavily indebted to Saxton's, and although his town plans are based on original surveys, they are not necessarily his own. Comparison of successive county maps will often reveal instances where one draws upon another, sometimes perpetuating errors.

Because of their scale, county maps rely upon symbols to depict buildings and coverage is usually limited to churches, seats of the aristocracy and gentry, and sometimes isolated buildings such as windmills and watermills that might constitute local landmarks. However, such maps can still furnish valuable information about roads and topographical features, such as parks, in periods for which larger-scale mapping is often unavailable. The same is generally true of road maps of the type pioneered by John Ogilby in his *Britannia* (1675), in which buildings and other topographical features bordering on main roads were depicted in a series of strip maps. John Speed adopted the expedient of placing larger-scale town maps (*see* Fig 2.2) in the margins of his county maps and this remained common practice throughout the 17th and 18th centuries, especially for county towns. The more generous depiction of county-wide detail was made possible by the adoption, from the mid-18th century onwards, of the 1-inch and 2-inch scales. Although even the most important buildings continued to be depicted symbolically, the larger scales enabled representation of a considerable amount of land-use information, including parkland, woodland, arable, pasture and common land, together with minor as well as major roads, rivers and bridges.

Town maps

Maps depicting towns in whole or in part survive in increasing numbers from the mid-16th century. Like county maps, some of the earliest were made for defence purposes and exist in manuscript form only (*see* Fig 1.9), but most served a variety of uses and were intended for publication and sale. The main sequence of maps for any given town is usually well known and copies can be consulted in local studies libraries, record offices and museums, but maps – particularly manuscript maps – held in private collections or national repositories, such as The National Archives (TNA) and the British Library (BL), are sometimes known only to specialist map historians. The fullest available listing is the Catalogue of British Town Maps (http://townmaps.data.history.ac.uk).

As with architectural drawings, different methods of pictorial representation prevailed at different periods in the production of town maps. Early bird's-eye views gave way to ichnographic or plan-view projections. On many of the latter, building elevations are depicted as though laid down flat. This practice continued into the 18th century but increasingly the depiction of building footprints became the norm. This may be seen as improving the metric standard of mapping but at the same time it entails a loss of valuable visual information. In the 18th century, perhaps compensating for this loss, the makers of town maps often incorporated marginal illustrations of notable buildings in the form of elevations or perspective views (Fig 2.1).

Particularly characteristic of 16th- and 17th-century mapping, bird's-eye views experienced a brief revival in the middle years of the 19th century, although primarily for their attractive pictorial qualities rather than for their usefulness as maps. Some were based on the view from a tethered balloon, although others adopted an imaginary rather than an actual viewpoint. Their particular value for architectural researchers lies in their representation of building layout and roof-level detail, as well as their rendering of ephemeral or other features not generally recorded by map-makers. In this they anticipate aerial photography.

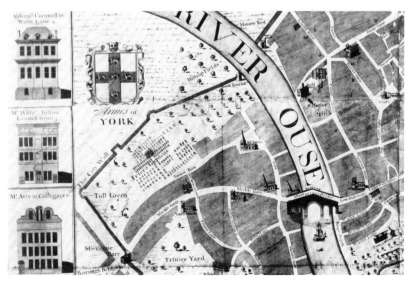

Fig 2.1
Detail from John Cossins *A New and Exact Plan of the City of York* (*c* 1727), showing the use of architectural elevations both on the map and in the margins. Many 18th-century cartographers adopted a similar approach.
[© Yorkshire Museums]

As a general rule, only major buildings such as churches, institutional buildings and the houses of the wealthy were portrayed on town maps with any specificity of detail. They are often still conventionalised, but certain features may be represented authentically (Fig 2.2). Lesser buildings tend to be represented by ciphers which give an impression of the nature of housing (one or two storeys, closely packed or more dispersed), but little more. Manuscript maps sometimes use a range of colours to denote different building materials. Rather than assume that these are based on observation instead of just a general indication of variety, compare the map with surviving fabric evidence, or consider whether they conform to a pattern.

Most town maps take more trouble with the administrative and commercial centre than they do with outlying areas, particularly if the latter contain no buildings of substance. It can therefore be dangerous to give too much weight to the precise depiction of outlying areas or the non-depiction of individual buildings. The problem was accentuated in the late 18th and early 19th centuries, when many towns experienced rapid expansion. Scaling problems arose as map-makers tried to include the new extent of a town, but also needed to represent the central business district legibly; one common solution was to omit fringe areas. Some town maps were reduced in scale to facilitate publication in a book, and as a result their detail is simplified (Fig 2.3a, 2.3b). When using such maps, it is worth ascertaining whether there is an original on a more generous scale.

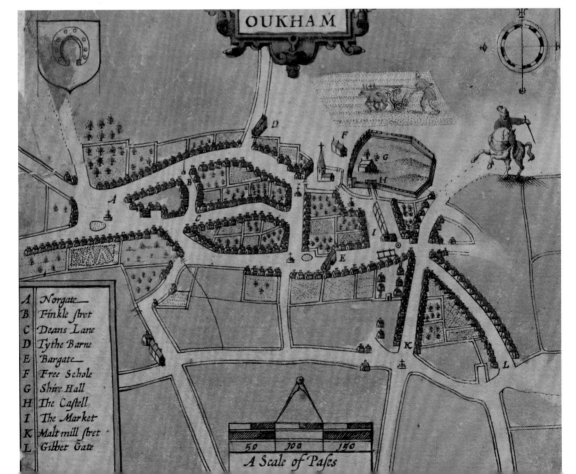

OUKHAM

A	Norgate
B	Finkle ſtret
C	Deans Lane
D	Tythe Barne
E	Bargate
F	Free Schole
G	Shire Hall
H	The Caſtell
I	The Market
K	Malt mill ſtret
L	Gilbet Gate

50   100   150

A Scale of Paſes

Fig. 2.3a
James Gillies' map of Blackburn, at the generous scale of about 20 inches to one mile (approx. 1:3168), was published as a single large sheet in 1822. This extract shows King St, the main street westwards from Blackburn, on which many merchants' houses were concentrated. For the accurate depiction of detail, and for the most reliable indication of the survey date, this should be the preferred version of the map. [© Royal Mail Group, courtesy of the Postal Museum 2018]

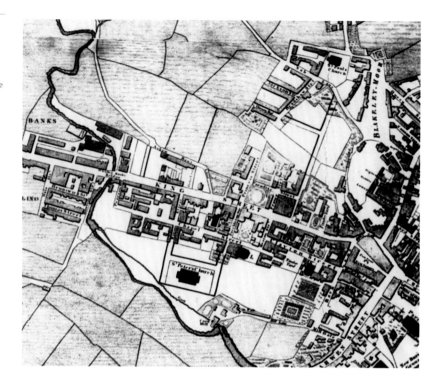

Fig. 2.3b
In 1824 a reduced version of Gillies' map was published in Edward Baines, *Lancashire Directory*, 1824–5. Designed to be printed on a single page of the directory, this version is much smaller than the original and simplifies the representation of building footprints (for example the buildings at the junction of King St and Byrom St). Although inscribed in the margin 'Surveyed, 1824', it is essentially a reduced copy of the earlier map, but it does include a series of projected streets, indicated by pecked lines, which are not shown on the original. Though inferior in its depiction of detail, therefore, this version nevertheless records valuable information which might elude the researcher who relied solely on the 1822 map. [Blackburn Central Library]

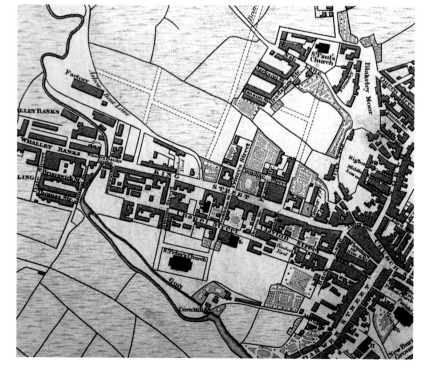

Maps in trade directories

When using maps to chart the development of a building or property the intervals between successive map editions can be frustrating. Before the modern era the nearest approach to continuously updated maps was provided by trade directories, some of which incorporated plans of major towns. In the largest towns and cities, such as Liverpool, new editions appeared annually or biennially. The maps included in directories fall far short of the standards of contemporary Ordnance Survey (OS) mapping but they can be used to establish whether a particular street existed, and sometimes they indicate the extent of building. Greater precision may be provided by an accompanying street directory.

Public health maps

A succession of public health scares in the first half of the 19th century focused the attention of municipalities and reformers on the need for improvements in the physical fabric of the nation's towns. In particular, drainage, ventilation and sanitation needed urgent remediation, as did elements of the existing housing stock, such as court housing, back-to-backs and cellar dwellings, considered injurious to health. Local Boards of Health, set up to address these challenges, commissioned surveys to quantify the problems and plan solutions (Fig 2.4).

The most important cartographic outcome of this endeavour was the production during the 1840s and 1850s, usually by the OS, of town maps produced specifically for Local Boards of Health. In order to display the required level of detail these maps were at large scales, such as 1:2640. As the OS began the more systematic coverage of towns at large scales the need for special public health maps diminished, but the importance of drainage and water quality continued to require the careful surveying of levels (particularly along streets) and wells, while the desire to effect improvements to highways and other areas of the public realm resulted in the minute documentation of features such as steps to entrances, area railings and cellar light-wells. In Berwick-upon-Tweed, on the OS map of 1855 at the scale of 1:528, ground levels are given inside buildings as well as on the roadway and can be used to identify the presence of cellars or basements.

Fig 2.4

A record of insanitary housing in Wallace Green, Berwick-upon-Tweed, from Robert Rawlinson, *Report to the General Board of Health on … the Sanitary Condition of the Inhabitants of the Parish of Berwick-upon-Tweed*, London, 1850. [Northumberland County Council, E26/7]

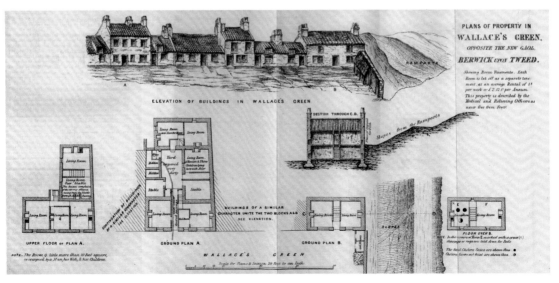

Some of these maps were not legally deposited and copies may be scarce. They are usually found in local record offices and archives. In some towns, where sanitary surveys were conducted or slum clearance programmes initiated, surveys of individual properties or areas were undertaken, and may survive among the records of the relevant Local Board of Health.

Goad insurance plans

These invaluable plans, generally at the very large scale of 1:480, were first compiled in 1885 by the Canadian firm of Charles E Goad Ltd (now Experian Goad) as a commercial undertaking for subscribers. They are listed in Rowley's *British Fire Insurance Plans* (1984). Their coverage corresponds to areas of high insurance value in larger towns – docks, commercial centres, and concentrations of industrial premises or warehousing – and they may deal very selectively or not at all with buildings in outlying areas. Some areas were surveyed once only, some were fully updated every few years, and others selectively updated by pasting revisions over a particular area.

Goad insurance plans employ an elaborate range of symbols to capture a huge quantity of detail, particularly features bearing on security and fire risk and prevention (Fig 2.5). The location of steam engines, boiler houses,

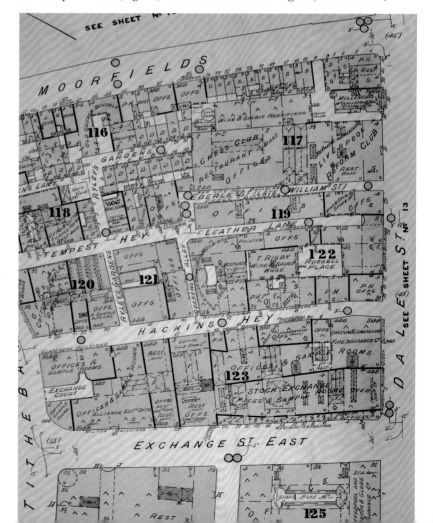

Fig 2.5
This extract from a Goad insurance plan of central Liverpool dating from 1888 shows a densely packed area of mostly commercial property. Colours denote different building materials. The maps must be read in conjunction with an elaborate key identifying many symbolic representations. [© Historic England Archive DP028665]

furnaces and electrical switchgear is abundantly indicated, as is the presence of iron or steel construction, fire-proof ceilings, fire doors and sprinkler systems. Colours are used to distinguish building materials (pink for brick, yellow for wood and blue for glass) and features such as doorways, windows and ventilation louvres are represented conventionally or by annotation. Later versions of the maps from the 1960s are much simplified and offer very little uniquely available information.

The British Library has the largest collection of Goad insurance plans for the British Isles, many of which can now be consulted digitally (http://www.bl.uk/onlinegallery/onlineex/firemaps/fireinsurancemaps.html). Local libraries and record offices often have local coverage.

Property maps

The principal purpose of a property map is to depict part or all of the property of a single owner (either private or institutional) or a number of owners. In most cases its main purpose is to verify boundaries and, through the more or less accurate depiction of land and other property, to facilitate management. In the case of an estate map it may have the additional benefit of conferring prestige on the owner whose property is displayed, and in some cases this may even have been the primary motive behind its creation.

Estate maps

Estate maps exist almost invariably in manuscript form because their use was confined to the owner and perhaps a steward or other official. Very occasionally a substantial owner might go to the expense of having maps engraved so that multiple copies could be distributed. Maps of compact estates are typically produced on a single sheet, but very large or scattered estates may be documented in a series of plans bound up to form an atlas (for example the printed map-books of the extensive Greenwich Hospital Estate). Most estate maps will be found in The National Archive, British Library and other major libraries, local record offices, and private, institutional and municipal archives (Fig 2.6). Many are attractively coloured and offer invaluable insights into past landscapes and buildings.

Deed plans

Until recently, title to property was established by the production of deeds that specified the property referred to and detailed its descent by will, sale or lease. By the 19th century it was common to include a map identifying the property by showing its boundaries, and usually any buildings on it, in relation to adjoining properties. Such plans provide a snapshot of the property at a given point in time. They are usually accompanied by written descriptions, although care must be taken in interpreting these, as they frequently employ conventional phrases and lists. Once large-scale OS maps were available the need for specially prepared deed plans declined, and by the late 19th century most deed plans were thinly disguised copies of OS 1:2500 or 1:10,560 mapping. There is therefore a risk that features may simply have been copied across from the OS map without regard to their actual existence at the date of the deed. For new properties, however, the need for a specially prepared plan remained.

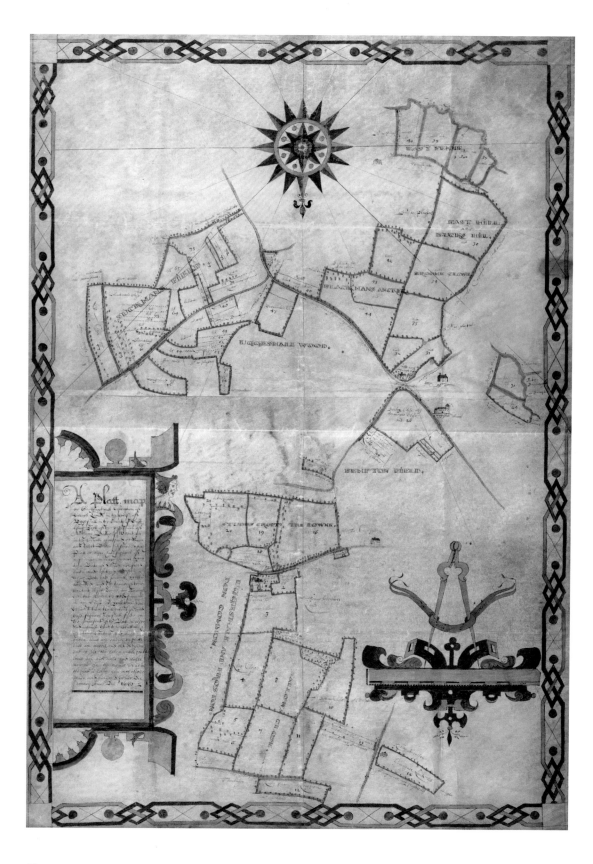

46

Many property deeds have found their way into record offices and archives but many more remain in private hands, where their future is uncertain. For this reason, wherever owners are willing, it is strongly recommended that researchers make careful notes of salient points and that they document photographically any specially prepared plans.

Sale particulars

Printed sale particulars became a common device for selling larger premises, businesses and estates during the 19th century, allowing more detailed descriptions than were economic in the advertisements carried by newspapers and journals. Early examples sometimes contain engraved views (Fig 2.7), and in the second half of the 19th century it became increasingly common to include reproductions of photographs. The engravings and photographs were often prepared specially for the sale and the originals have rarely survived. The existence of sale particulars is not necessarily proof of a sale. If buyers did not come forward, or if the asking price was not forthcoming, properties might be withdrawn.

Sale particulars vary considerably in detail. The most comprehensive give the names, dimensions and features of the rooms (sometimes with interior photographs), and descriptions of ancillary buildings, gardens and other land, as well as any industrial, farm and cottage property belonging to the house. Where the property is extensive they are usually accompanied by a map, either prepared specially for the particulars or derived from an existing (usually OS) map.

The survival of sale particulars is unpredictable. Through deliberate policies of acquisition many have found their way into archives, record offices, local studies libraries and the Historic England Archive. Some remain in record offices, among solicitors' papers or the papers of the family that bought or sold the property, but sometimes they crop up in other collections – kept perhaps by a prospective purchaser or by someone with a local interest in the house. The emergence of web-based finding aids such as those produced by The National Archives has greatly increased the chances of locating these 'strays'.

Cadastral maps

In the past, the term 'cadastral map' was restricted to maps made for purposes of taxation, but in contemporary usage it refers to all maps covering an administrative area, regardless of ownership. The types most commonly used by historians are enclosure maps and tithe maps, both of which are normally encountered in manuscript form.

Enclosure maps

Enclosure maps were commissioned as part of schemes (either by Act of Parliament or by voluntary agreement among landowners and communities) to enclose common land, whether in open fields or uncultivated 'wastes'. From the 16th century to the early 20th century such schemes formed part of a protracted process whereby communal rights were translated into rights of private ownership and the face of the land was transformed. Maps were required so that allocations of land to individuals or institutions could be made proportionate to their pre-enclosure holdings and common rights. Pre- and post-enclosure maps were the best way of ensuring that these principles were observed, and where both survive, the appearance or disappearance of individual features depicted on one map but not on the other, can be dated very precisely (Fig 2.8a, 2.8b). More commonly only the post-enclosure map survives, and the survival even of these is rare for early schemes. The scale of enclosure maps varies considerably, but most are at scales larger than 6 inches to 1 mile (1:10,560).

Enclosure maps were made primarily to establish acreages and they do not always depict buildings systematically, sometimes omitting village centres. Buildings and other topographical features are included only because they help to identify individual parcels of land by providing familiar landmarks and context. Minutely accurate depictions of buildings are therefore not to be expected, but the need to depict individual buildings and groups of buildings recognisably, coupled with an attachment to certain conventions and standards of mapping, must have persuaded many surveyors to render salient points and relationships with reasonable precision. Many enclosure maps can be consulted in record offices, but some have found their way into other collections.

Tithe maps

Tithe maps were made in fulfilment of the terms of the Tithe Commutation Act, 1836, which brought to an end the ancient practice of payment of tithes in kind, replacing it with a system of monetary payments based on acreages of eligible land. Tithe maps were produced in large numbers in England and Wales, in a once-only exercise between 1837 and 1850. Although governed by national legislation and overseen by a national body – the Tithe Commissioners – the commissioning of tithe maps was left to individual parishes and townships, which employed a multitude of independent surveyors. The Tithe Commissioners advocated standards for content, depiction and accuracy, but were not empowered to enforce them, with the result that tithe maps vary considerably. The scales also vary, with large parishes or townships often surveyed at smaller scales than small parishes.

Tithe maps were always accompanied by a written schedule of property, numbered parcel by parcel, together with acreages, land use, titheable value, owners, lessees and occupiers. The map and schedule once held by the Tithe

Fig 2.8a
Pre- and post-enclosure maps of
the village of Oxborough, Norfolk.
The earlier map (reproduced
inverted for ease of comparison)
is titled 'An Exact Survey of the
Parish of Oxburgh in the County of
Norfolk ... Survey'd Anno Domini
1722 by Philip Wissiter', and was
probably made in anticipation of
a private enclosure Act of 1724.
[Norfolk Record Office, BRA
2524/1]

Fig 2.8b
The post-enclosure map was
surveyed by I de Wilstar 'Ingineer
& Architecte' in 1725 and exists
in two states (Norfolk Record
Office, BRA 2524/2 [reproduced]
and BRA 2524/3). Comparison
of the 1722 and 1725 maps
reveals not only the enclosure
of formerly open arable land,
but the establishment of a new
formal approach to Oxburgh
Hall (moated, left of centre) and
significant changes to the gardens.
There is also a shift from laid-flat
elevations to plan representations
of buildings. [Norfolk Record
Office, BRA 2524/2]

Commissioners can now be found in The National Archives; the parish or township copy of each is generally held by the relevant record office; a third copy went to the diocese. Rates of survival are very high, with the result that tithe maps provide almost national, large-scale coverage of England up to a decade before the OS began surveying at large scales on the British mainland, and nearly 50 years before some counties were first surveyed at 1:2500 by the OS.

Like enclosure maps, the primary purpose of tithe maps was to establish acreages accurately, although most depict buildings with a reasonable attention to detail. A common failing of tithe maps, however, is that areas of non-titheable land (often in urban areas) and their associated buildings are frequently omitted.

Many tithe maps have been digitised and some have had their schedules transcribed to make them searchable and are viewable online: see for example the Kent Tithe Maps (www.kentarchaeology.org.uk).

Ordnance Survey maps

The foundation of the OS is generally dated to 1793, although its origins go back to the Military Survey of Scotland in the 1750s and 1760s. Its purposes were initially purely military, although from an early date maps were sold to the general public and a range of civil uses for them quickly emerged. From the 1790s the OS compiled maps county by county for engraving and publication at the scale of 1 inch to 1 mile (1:63,360). The 6-inch scale (1:10,560) was first introduced in Ireland in 1824, and adopted on the British mainland from 1841. During the 1850s the much larger 1:2500 scale (roughly 25 inches to 1 mile) was launched, eventually covering the majority of the British Isles. Larger scales were restricted to urban areas. Ordnance Survey maps were made by professional surveyors working to broadly consistent, although gradually evolving, conventions. Standards of planimetric accuracy sometimes faltered but the depiction of detail is generally highly reliable. Although some errors are inevitable, it is worth considering other explanations carefully before concluding that an OS map is at fault.

Larger-scale OS maps have always been published on 'sheet lines', which serve to divide a county or town into a number of sheets of consistent size; latterly sheet lines have been in conformity with the National Grid lines. Early sheets stop at county boundaries, with the result that some sheets contain only a small area of mapping at the margin. However, certain details beyond the boundary are sometimes shown, particularly water features (eg the opposite side of rivers or lakes forming or straddling county boundaries). Later editions provide uniform coverage regardless of administrative boundaries. In either case it is worth checking maps of the adjacent county, which are likely to have been surveyed at a different date and may therefore allow dating to be refined. Users of these maps in digital format will be alerted to their existence by the presence of overlapping 'tiles'.

There are marked differences in presentation and utility between the various scales used by the OS at different periods of its history. What follows considers the most important historic scales but is not exhaustive. Further information is provided by Oliver 2013 (3 edn) *Ordnance Survey Maps: A Concise Guide for Historians*.

OS editions

Most OS maps carry, usually on the lower margin, the date of survey or revision and the date of publication, sometimes supplemented by other information such as a date of reprinting, or a scale bar and key. For most purposes the date of survey or last revision is the key date for historians, but recording the date of publication as well guards against the possibility of further piecemeal revisions having been incorporated prior to printing. Where the date of survey or publication is lacking it can sometimes be found by referring to a later edition of the same map sheet.

Regrettably, marginal data are often absent from digitised copies of maps, their omission facilitating the continuous 'tiling' of a series of sheets. Even when using original paper maps, however, care is needed when assigning dates to individual features. Reprints of maps are not always distinguished clearly from the original editions, and railways and other major changes in the landscape were sometimes added after the stated date of publication in order to extend a map's currency. A cautious approach is therefore to record any indication that the map copy being used is a reprint (often stated in the bottom left corner) and to seek opportunities to compare earlier copies.

From the 1860s, amid heightened fears of invasion, militarily sensitive sites and adjacent contour information were routinely omitted from maps for public use, but uncensored War Office editions can be found in The National Archives (eg, WO 78). Descriptions of industrial plant were omitted (the term 'Works' was used instead) from 1915, and gas works were omitted entirely, but the policy was relaxed after the First World War.

OS maps, particularly at the smaller scales, were produced in relatively large quantities, although the public demand for some large-scale sheets must have been very small indeed. There are very full sets in the British Library and other legal deposit libraries; the set belonging to the OS itself suffered losses to wartime bombing but is still very large. Record offices and local history libraries generally have good or near-complete sets for their area, as do some estate offices.

Increasing numbers of OS maps are now available online, subject to the caveats noted above. Staff and students of participating institutions can use EDINA Digimap® (http://digimap.edina.ac.uk/digimap/) hosted by the University of Edinburgh, which covers the whole of Great Britain and the Isle of Man. The National Library of Scotland's online coverage of Great Britain is not yet complete for England and Wales, but has the great advantage of presenting the maps with map-edge data intact (http://maps.nls.uk/).

The 1-inch series

Most of the early activity of the OS was focused on the production of maps at the scale of 1 inch to 1 mile (1:63,360). This scale is too small to permit the precise depiction of buildings, but because for some decades no larger-scale maps were published by the OS the series is worth consulting, especially where the landscape context is of interest. Of special value are the Ordnance Surveyors' drawings which were drafted (but never published), usually at the larger scale of 2 inches to 1 mile (1:31,680). These were made from the 1780s until 1840, depending on when the OS was at work in a given locality, and survive in the British Library for most of England and Wales south of Liverpool and Hull. They can be viewed at http://www.bl.uk/onlinegallery/onlineex/ordsurvdraw/.

The County Series 6-inch maps

Maps at 1:10,560, or 6 inches to 1 mile, were first introduced in England in the 1840s; by about 1890 the whole country had been surveyed and a process of complete revision began. The earliest 6-inch maps, such as those of Lancashire and Yorkshire, were surveyed at this scale, but once mapping at 1:2500 commenced in the 1850s new 6-inch maps were derived from the 1:2500 surveys. In theory this should make the smaller scale redundant for most historical purposes wherever copies of the 1:2500 mapping are available, but in practice they provide useful information of their own. Unlike 1:2500 maps, they provide truly national coverage, including areas consisting predominantly of moorland that were not mapped at the larger scale. Also, unlike the larger scale, they show contours, allowing the physical setting of buildings to be visualised; they also sometimes annotate features that are not annotated on the larger-scale maps, or annotate them differently in ways that can occasionally furnish additional evidence. As aids to dating, 6-inch maps can be frustrating. Because most were compiled from 1:2500 sheets, the date of survey across the whole 6-inch sheet (or quarter-sheet) can span a number of years, and there is no indication on the map itself as to which part was surveyed at which date. For dating purposes, therefore, preference should always be given to the 1:2500 mapping, if available.

The quality of engraving of 19th-century 1:10,560 maps is extremely high, allowing dimensions to be derived from them with a fair degree of accuracy (perhaps ±1m). This quality quickly diminishes with copying or scanning. Every effort should therefore be made to consult original copies. The depiction of some details on this and larger scales may be more precise than map users imagine. Trees forming lines, avenues or boundaries, individual hedgerow trees and prominent isolated trees were all at various times surveyed to varying degrees of accuracy.

The County Series 1:2500 maps

Almost all the enclosed land of England and Wales was mapped at the 1:2500 scale between 1853 and 1896, concluding with those counties that had been the first to be mapped at 1:10,560. Thereafter, sheets were revised between one and four times up to the 1940s, with urban and suburban areas (where the pace of change was most rapid) typically receiving the most frequent attention.

Nearly all first edition 1:2500 sheets were produced in both monochrome and hand-coloured versions (Fig 2.9). Where possible, use of the latter is strongly recommended, as they are less prone to misinterpretation. Roads, water and structures are coloured; most buildings are coloured carmine (pink); timber, iron and mud-walled buildings are coloured grey and glass-roofed structures have cross-hatching and blue wash. In practice the definition of timber buildings evidently did not include most historic timber-framed buildings, and the identification of mud-walled buildings is likely to have been patchy. Large trees were accurately plotted and are distinguished by having a shadow shown at the intersection of trunk and ground.

As with other map scales, detailed instructions were issued from time to time, covering what was and was not to be surveyed. Of particular note for the representation of buildings is the fact that greater precision was employed where an elevation abutted a public thoroughfare than elsewhere. In 1905, for example, guidelines specified that projections less than 2m deep on 1:2500 maps should be ignored where they did not adjoin public land. This resulted in many bay windows being omitted.

Fig 2.9

An example of the clarity and

attractiveness of the coloured

version of OS 1:2500 mapping: the

hamlet of Town End, Grasmere,

Cumbria. [The Bodleian Libraries.

The University of Oxford, OS 25

1st ed, Westmorland, Grasmere,

Sheet XXVI.1]

OS town plans

The systematic mapping of towns at very large scales (1:1250, 1:1056, 1:528 and 1:500) commenced in the 1840s. The 1:1056 scale (5ft = 1 mile) was the first to be adopted, but was largely superseded from 1850 by the more generous 1:528 scale (10ft = 1 mile), which was in turn replaced from 1855 by 1:500 maps. Coverage was largely confined to towns whose population at the time of survey exceeded 4,000 inhabitants; a small number of county towns with populations below this limit were also surveyed. The principal exception was London, which was mapped twice at 1:1056, but never at the larger scales.

A particularly valuable feature of many OS town plans is the depiction of the internal arrangements of public buildings, including door and window positions, room names and, in churches and some other buildings, seating plans. They are also particularly valuable for their depiction of detailed garden layouts of even quite modest properties, as well as public parks, street furniture and other elements of the public realm.

After 1910 the very large mapping scales were not employed again, and the special treatment of larger towns did not resume until the Second World War. The 1:1250 scale became the standard scale for mapping larger towns on National Grid lines from 1943. These maps now have historic value in their own right, and can be particularly useful for their inclusion of street numbering and a greater range of house names than earlier maps.

Research questions for historic maps

In many important respects the critical scrutiny of maps follows the same lines as those recommended when looking at architectural drawings, but there are a number of specific issues of importance.

When was the map made? Most maps carry a date, and some separately specify the date of survey, but some maps are datable only stylistically, by reference to named individuals, or to what they do and do not depict.

Does the map exist in a number of different states or editions? This might be a manuscript version of a printed map, or the field measurements on which the map was based. Information on successive revisions or editions may be documented in carto-bibliographies.

What was the map made for? Is the accurate depiction of buildings, or of other features of interest, relevant to the map's purpose? What might this suggest about the accuracy and reliability of the map in its treatment of different landscape features?

On what principle was the map drawn? This might be profile, bird's-eye, elevated bird's-eye, or ichnographic (plan view).

Is it the outcome of actual survey? Was the survey specifically undertaken for this map or is some or all of the information compiled from other sources?

Is it drawn to a consistent scale? If so, what scale is it, and what limitations does this scale impose?

Are features delineated consistently? Is the same level of detail given across the whole area of the map, or does it diminish in certain areas (eg towards the margins, or in densely built-up areas)?

Are buildings and other features of interest shown symbolically, pictorially or by plan footprint? If they are shown pictorially, do they attempt to render specific characteristics? If they are depicted by footprint, do they show the internal plan, the actual footprint in solid form or a generalised impression (such as area hatching)?

What information is offered by annotation? Are individual buildings or other features of interest identifiable by their names or by owners or occupiers?

Is there a key? Are the symbols and/or colours or other conventions used on the map identified in a key? If not, can their meaning be inferred from the map and from comparison with other material?

Is (or was) the map accompanied by separate written material? This might be in the form of letterpress, a schedule, register, apportionment or field book. What does this add to the information contained in the map, or how does its absence limit interpretation?

Has drawn or written information been added to the map after it was first completed? If so, when, by whom and for what purpose?

3 | Topographical views

This chapter discusses topographical views produced in circumstances other than an architect's or landscape designer's professional involvement with a particular property or development. Some views were commissioned by owners to show off their property; some were taken as personal mementoes of a visit, or in the pursuit of antiquarian knowledge; and some were undertaken with a view to publication and sale.

During the 18th century, there was a dramatic increase in the production of topographical views by both amateurs and professionals in oil and watercolour, typically worked up subsequently from sketches made at the scene. The increase was spurred by the growth of domestic tourism, which had been facilitated by improvements in roads and was fuelled by the desire to take advantage of the intellectual and social benefits of seeing new places without the inconveniences and expense of foreign travel. Tourists compiled sketchbooks and even their sometimes naive renderings can provide valuable visual documentation (Fig 3.1). Tourists also created a market for images of landscapes and buildings, and itinerant 'view takers' produced original drawings or paintings that can offer information about existing or now lost buildings and features. Depictions by both trained and untrained artists were strongly influenced by the aesthetic of 'The Picturesque', a mode of viewing which judged the qualities of landscape on the basis of its suitability for

Fig 3.1
Nappa Hall, Askrigg, North Yorkshire, is a substantial stone manor house of c 1470. Samuel James Allen's 1846 drawing records a number of details – such as the door inserted in one of the hall windows – not apparent on earlier or later views but corroborating evidence preserved in the building's fabric. [© City of York Libraries, Archives and Local History 100/SO1/096 www.york.gov.uk/archives]

composing a picture. Typical elements are framing devices (such as trees), gentle asymmetry and figures introduced into the scene ('staffage'). The likely exercise of artistic licence should always be considered when using such images as evidence: viewpoints were frequently chosen so as to mask features judged 'unpicturesque', such as recent buildings, or the service ranges of large houses.

With increasing commercial demand for views of notable buildings, either as separate prints or bound into books, artists were emboldened to make views specifically with a view to engraving and publication. This means that most printed views exist (or once existed) in a number of states: the artist's original view (which would often be redrawn or painted to produce a final version), the print-maker's block and the published print. Naturally the artist's view

Fig 3.2a
These two views of Oxburgh Hall, Norfolk, are unusual in representing the courtyard face of the gatehouse (nearly all views of Oxburgh show the outer face). An inscription notes that the first (3.2a) was 'Drawn from Nature & in Stone [ie lithography] by Joseph Nash Pupil to A Pugin'; it was published by Pugin in 1830 and reprinted in Nash's *The Mansions of England in the Olden Time* (4 vols, 1838–1849), where the views are characteristically presented with 'period' figures and costumes. Despite being drawn from nature and engraved by the artist himself the view takes liberties with the subject: the single-storey range bottom left dates from 1775–1779 and was built with a plain, not crenelated parapet; the doorway, shown by Nash as a late-medieval opening, dates in this form only from 1829–1830; a convenient and probably fictitious tree obviates the need for similar 'artistic' retouching of a matching single-storey range to the right. [© Historic England Archive XA00273]

will normally be closer to the building, landscape or other feature, in terms of accurate observation, than the version prepared by a print-maker who may never have seen the subject of his work (although some artists, like Hollar in the 17th century, the brothers Samuel and Nathaniel Buck in the 18th century, and John Sell Cotman in the 19th century, produced their own prints). But even the artist may simplify, elaborate, misinterpret or omit detail, distort proportions carelessly or to produce a calculated effect, or rearrange elements to achieve a more powerful (but less accurate) composition. A print-maker may perpetrate similar distortions, and may also crop or expand the view (Fig 3.2a, 3.2b). The resulting print will inevitably be conditioned to some degree by the method of print-making employed and the pictorial fashions of the day.

Fig 3.2b
The second view, this time a steel engraving, was printed in 1859 in volume 3 of J H Parker & T Hudson Turner, *Some Account of Domestic Architecture in England* (4 vols, 1851–1859) but the engraver, identified on the plate as J H Le Keux (1783–1846), had by then been dead more than a decade. The artist's name is not given but may be Frederick Mackenzie (1787–1854). Comparison with Nash's view reveals that Le Keux (or the artist) removes later excrescences from the view, with the result that the single-storey ranges do not appear at all. Rather than insert possibly misleading detail in the walls thus revealed, the engraving leaves them blank, but the dormer window is a 'medievalised' interpretation of an existing window. [© Historic England Archive RBA01/15/008/01]

Engraving techniques

There are a number of ways in which illustrative material has been prepared for publication, and different techniques are sometimes combined on the same print. Each method has its own characteristics and limitations; some were in use for relatively restricted periods, making them approximately datable in the absence of more precise evidence; others have long histories, but within which certain stylistic trends can be discerned. A full guide to the identification of processes can be found in Gascoigne (2004), but it is worth stressing that identification may be difficult or impossible if consulting a secondary reproduction of the print. The following techniques are most commonly used for architectural subjects.

Relief processes

In relief processes the positive printed image is produced by a raised surface, the other parts of the printer's block having been cut away. The block is inked and printed: the recessed areas are ink-free and therefore blank, while the protruding elements carry ink and create the image.

Woodcuts, in which the image is cut into the broad face of the wood, have been produced since the 16th century. They generally create a coarser image and are limited in their ability to convey precise detail (Fig 3.3).

Wood engraving uses the end-grain of a dense wood (usually boxwood) and achieves much finer results. The technique was widely used throughout the 19th century for illustrations set within the text rather than interleaved as separate 'plates'.

Fig 3.3
An unsigned woodcut prospect of Leeds. Both the printing technique and the skill with perspective of the artist/engraver impose severe limitations on the value of the resulting image as a record source. Nevertheless some features, including three churches, are recognisable. Compare Fig 3.4. [Author's collection. From Gent, Thomas 1733 *The antient and modern history of the loyal town of Rippon*. York]

Intaglio processes

Intaglio processes are the opposite of relief processes. The image is made by incising lines into the surface of a metal plate. The plate is then inked: the ink sinks into the incised lines and the plate is wiped clean. The plate is then applied to the paper under pressure, squeezing the ink out of the incisions and leaving an indented plate mark around the image.

Copper engraving, the standard technique for high-quality line engraving in the 17th and 18th centuries (Fig 3.4), was largely replaced by steel engraving from the 1820s.

Steel engraving, first widely used for print-making in the 1820s, employs finer, more closely spaced lines than copper engraving, giving considerable tonal depth overall and a silvery sheen to the lighter areas such as sky (Fig 3.5).

Etching involves coating the plate with a wax ground before incising the design. The plate is then dipped in acid, which bites into the plate. This is repeated to create incisions of differing depths – the deeper the incision the darker the resulting image. The ground is removed prior to inking and printing. Etching produces greater subtleties of tone than line engraving.

Aquatint was devised to produce an effect comparable to that of watercolour. Here the action of the acid on the plate is impeded to varying degrees by the application of resin, producing a subtly graded tone and soft effect in the printed image. The process was popularised by Paul Sandby in the 1770s and remained fashionable until the 1830s (Fig 3.6).

Fig 3.4
A nearly contemporary (1745) view, but this time a copperplate engraving of 'The South-East Prospect of Leeds' by Samuel and Nathaniel Buck. The handling of perspective and the familiarity with architectural features combine with the ability of copper to render very precise details to create an image packed with observation. The church top right is St John's, which appears top left (on the skyline) in the Gent woodcut (Fig 3.3). [By kind permission of West Yorkshire Archive Service, ACC 4180]

Fig 3.5 (opposite)
Steel engraving of St John the Baptist, Windlesham, Surrey, by E Radclyffe (1809–1863) after Thomas Allom (1804–1872), a prolific topographical artist. The church was restored by the architect R Ebbels in 1838; he and the incumbents presented the engraving for inclusion in Edward Wedlake Brayley's *Topographical History of Surrey* (5 vols, Dorking & London, 1841–1848). [Author's collection]

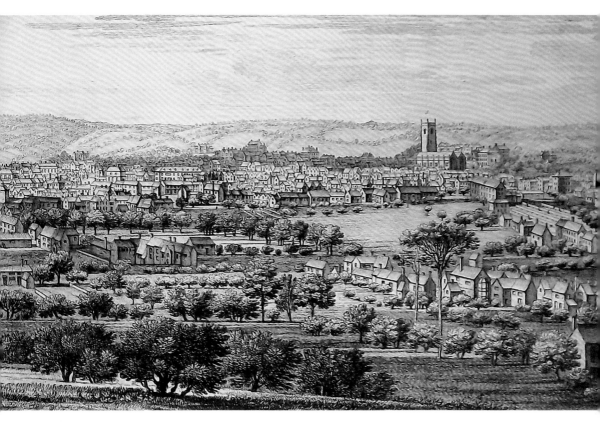

Mezzotints were produced from the mid-17th century onwards. Unlike the other methods which work from light to dark, mezzotint works from dark to light. The process involves roughening the whole plate, then smoothing portions selectively to produce the image. Mezzotint produces a richness of tone and depth and is ideally suited to portraying texture and shadow.

Planographic processes

Lithography relies not on the production of a raised or indented surface, but on transferring the design to a stone block (usually limestone) using a greasy crayon that repels ink. Richness of tone can be provided by making a second impression with a tint stone, giving an overall colour wash. Lithography was invented in Germany in 1798 but little used in Britain before 1818. Thereafter it enjoyed a prolonged vogue, especially for topographical and architectural subjects.

Chromolithography uses a series of stones to build up a multicoloured design.

Dating topographical views

The commercial potential of an image will often have depended on its being up to date, and many views were certainly swiftly engraved and published. Either a delay in working up a sketch or the vagaries of the print publishing market, however, meant that sometimes a number of years passed between the production of the original artwork and the publication of the print. It is therefore advisable, whenever working from a print, to see whether the artist's original work, whether surviving or not, can be identified, and if so, whether it can be dated. Once engraved, a publisher's plate represented a substantial investment in labour and materials and might remain in use for some years unless it became worn out through excessive use. Equally, finished prints might be held by a publisher for a considerable time, especially if they did not sell briskly, and could be bound into later publications for which they were not originally intended. Moreover, prints were sometimes copied by publishers, even many years after their first publication. A comparison of the different versions will normally reveal clear differences.

The problems of dating prints are eased somewhat after 1777, when the Prints Copyright Act guaranteed the rights of proprietors and required them, *inter alia*, to record the date of publication on the margin of the print. Where this information is absent the identities of the artist and engraver may help to refine dating. Prints normally bear the names of both. The originating artist is usually distinguished by the Latin 'delineavit' (abbreviated to 'del.'), and the engraver is distinguished by the term 'sculpsit' (abbreviated to 'sculp.' or 'sc.'). The vital dates of many engravers can be identified from reference works, and the careers of some artists have been chronicled in great detail, allowing views to be linked in some cases with a known sketching tour.

Care should be taken in interpreting the coloration of features depicted in prints, many of which have been coloured subsequently in an attempt to enhance their value. Even where prints were hand coloured prior to sale the colourist is likely to have had no direct knowledge of the subject.

Sources of topographical views

There are many collections of architectural and topographical views in museums, galleries and other repositories. Among the most useful are:

The British Library (online searchable gallery: www.bl.uk/onlinegallery/index. html) including the King George III Topographical Collection (selection of images viewable at http://www.bl.uk/onlinegallery/onlineex/kinggeorge)

The National Archives – see their Architectural Drawings research guide for detailed holdings (http://www.nationalarchives.gov.uk/records/research-guides/architectural-drawings.htm)

Historic England Archive (online catalogue: http://archive.historicengland.org.uk)

V&A + RIBA Architecture Partnership (online catalogue: http://riba.sirsidynix.net.uk/uhtbin/webcat)

Bodleian Library (http://www.bodleian.ox.ac.uk/)

Research questions for topographical views

Who made the view? In the case of prints, the artist, the engraver and the print-maker may all be different people, which may impact on the accuracy of the image as a record.

For whom, and for what purpose, was the view made? Does it record a particular moment, such as imminent demolition or recent completion of the building? Does it relate to a specific design, either as a proposal or as a record?

What medium does it employ: pencil, watercolour, oil, print? If it is a print, one must consider by what process it was produced, which can be indicative of its purpose and date, and whether an original painting or sketch survives.

What is its date? When was the original view taken and, for a print, when was it first published? Is it dated explicitly? Can it be dated by reference to other sources? For a print, does the technique employed help to date it? Is there internal evidence allowing the date to be narrowed to a span of years? For example, does the view include any features whose appearance or disappearance at or by a particular date can be verified from other sources?

Does the depiction of details suggest that the artist was an accurate and knowledgeable observer? Be aware that ostensible accuracy can be simply visual rhetoric. Both amateurs and artists made topographical views, and their priorities may be reflected in the depiction of the building and its setting. Where possible the view should be compared with other sources or with the built fabric and garden or landscape itself to evaluate.

Is the view part of a larger series of related images or a publication with accompanying letterpress? These textual sources may contribute to our understanding of the view.

4 | Additional visual sources

Models

The use of architectural models – both of whole buildings and of details –
is documented in antiquity and the medieval period, although few pre-
Renaissance models survive. In *De Architettura Libri Decem*, Vitruvius
mentioned the use of models by architects for planning projects and
presenting schemes. Likewise, in *De Re Aedificatoria* (1485), Alberti
recommended the use of models by architects for refining their ideas.
Surviving evidence of the use of architectural models in England only
dates to the 17th century. Henry Wotton made the first known reference
to architectural models in England in his *Elements of Architecture* (1624),
advising that no patron should commence work without making 'a Modell or
Type of the whole structure, and of every particular in Pastboard or Wood'.
The word 'model' did not, however, always mean a three-dimensional
rendering. It could also refer to a complete architectural design that was
drawn on paper, so a textual reference to a 'model' may not necessarily
indicate that a three-dimensional scaled object existed.

Architectural models, like drawings, can be used to represent a
building at various stages of realisation: during the design process, to guide
construction itself, or to record a completed building, either for posterity
or prior to alterations. It is possible to identify numerous types of model:
the conceptual model produced independent of practical consideration;
the experimental model created to address specific design problems; the
presentation model generated for a client, committee, competition jury or
the general public; the working model for use by the builder or the architect's
deputies; the record model created to document a completed project; the site
model for conveying the context of a group of buildings; the didactic model
for the architectural student; and the display model for the collector, such
as the cork models of ancient temples collected by Sir John Soane. As with
other visual sources, when using an architectural model the specific purpose
it was intended for and what stage of realisation it represents should both
be considered. Actual models in all periods were also intended to be used
in conjunction with drawings, and should be considered alongside each
other, where both exist. In some cases, models may be the only surviving
representation of an unrealised scheme.

As with drawings, models can provide useful evidence of the evolution of
a building. Christopher Wren's Great Model, for example, which includes the
interior detailing of carving and plasterwork, manifests his most ambitious
design for St Paul's (Fig 4.1). The model was commissioned after Charles II
had given his approval to the design and the Royal Warrant declared that
the model would 'remain as a perpetual unchangeable Rule and Direction
for the conduct of the whole work'. In the event, however, sight of the model
alarmed the conservative Dean and Chapter, leading to modifications.
Likewise, the model for Hawksmoor's Easton Neston shows an earlier design,

Fig 4.1

The 'Great Model' for St Paul's
Cathedral, 1673–74, seen from
the north west, in the cathedral's
Trophy Room, where it was first
displayed in 1709. Designed by
Sir Christopher Wren in 1673,
and built in oak and pear wood
by William Clere, to a scale of 2ft
to 1in (1:24). It measures 20ft
11in long (6.36m.), 13ft 1in wide
(3.97m.) and 13ft high (3.95m.).
[© The Chapter of St Paul's
Cathedral]

which was altered in the course of building. Models should be compared with
other sources, including drawings and documents and the building itself to
establish their place in the design process.

Models can be made from a variety of materials, although most are
typically cardboard or wood. From the 19th century, wax, plaster and
papier mâché were also employed. Models are often delicate and therefore
survive in a fragile condition, if at all. Like working drawings, working
models are susceptible to destruction by use, and are therefore more scarce.
The level of detail in a model depends to a large extent on what stage of
realisation it corresponds to (Fig 4.2). Painted models are in effect similar
to the presentation drawing. Prior to the 19th century, models were most
often constructed by cabinetmakers. In the 19th century models were made
by professional model-makers and, although in the early 20th century
they were usually constructed in the architect's office, from the mid-1950s
professionals again came to the fore.

Models were, and continue to be, constructed for various reasons.
One of their advantages is that they allow the architect to experiment
in three dimensions without the expense of actually building. They also
offer a way of conveying all the aspects of a building at once, rather than
in a series of separate drawings. Models are also useful for representing

the architect's ideas in situations where a three-dimensional expression might be more effective than a two-dimensional drawing – either to give patrons a holistic impression of a scheme, to impart specific technical information to workmen, or to convey information to those unaccustomed to reading elevations, plans and sections. During the 19th century models were recognised as useful not only for architect and client but for public consultation. Many critics felt that a model was more revealing of a proposed building than a perspective drawing, which could misrepresent its effect, and therefore recommended that all public works should be displayed in model form. In the 19th century, models were also displayed at exhibitions celebrating engineering and architectural innovation, such as international exhibitions, and at the Royal Academy.

Fig 4.2

This presentation model of Pitt House, Chudleigh Knighton, Devon, was prepared for Thomas Pinsent in 1841 by architects Scott & Moffat. It allowed the patron to consider the overall effect of the design, and even came in its own travelling case. [© RIBA Collections, MOD/SCOT/1]

Books of designs and pattern books

Of paramount importance in the dissemination of architectural styles in the 18th and early 19th centuries were books of designs and pattern books. Both types of publication focus on providing visual material and do not contain text other than the author's introduction and a brief description of the plates. Books of designs, the first British example of which is Colen Campbell's *Vitruvius Britannicus* (1715, 1717, 1725), were a way for the author/architect to promote his work, assert his status and set an agenda for architectural style. They therefore feature executed designs or designs that were unexecuted but drawn up for a specific, often prestigious, project. Pattern books are different in that they present a collection of possible, ideal designs from which the reader could draw inspiration for their own project. They therefore present multiple alternative solutions, either on different scales, or in different styles, in order to help the reader make a choice. Such titles include Batty Langley's *The City and Country Builder's Treasury of Designs* (1740) and William Halfpenny's *Useful Architecture in Twenty-One New Designs for Erecting Parsonage-Houses, Farm-Houses, and Inns* (1752) (Fig 4.3). Books of designs and pattern books were used by established and aspiring architects, builders, craftsmen and their patrons. They were a major vehicle for transmitting

Fig 4.3

Plate 1 from William Halfpenny's pattern book *Useful Architecture in Twenty-One New Designs* shows a generic design for a parsonage or an inn. The book was so popular that it went through six editions. [University of Wisconsin]

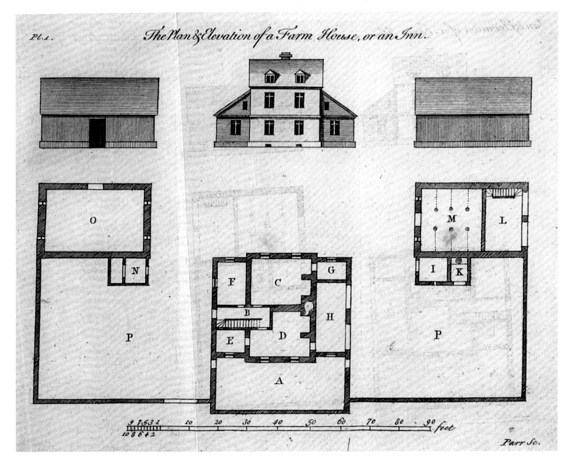

designs and fashions from skilled designers to less experienced ones. Their use in a building can sometimes be detected through identifying specific features, or their influence might be suggested by the presence of a copy in the house's library (if contemporary). Evidence of their use helps to explain the design process of a project and suggests the taste and aspirations of the patron. Many can be examined in digital form via Eighteenth Century Collections Online (ECCO).

Guidebooks

The earliest printed guidebooks date from the 18th century and were produced for numerous county towns and cities, for a number of country houses and their gardens, and for emerging tourist destinations such as the Lake District. During the 19th century such titles proliferated enormously. They were sometimes illustrated with maps, engravings of individual buildings and views of towns. The discussions above regarding these individual sources are therefore all relevant when drawing out information from guidebooks. Guidebooks are particularly useful for documenting the development of a given place and comparing successive editions of the same text can sometimes help to pinpoint the date of buildings. The focus of their attention was not only on buildings that were notable to the visitor for their antiquity, but also on buildings that had been recently erected and indicated the town's contemporary wealth and status. They are therefore useful sources about manufactories, hospitals and public buildings. Many guidebooks were published locally and copies may be held in local archives. Some can be found in digital form via ECCO; an especially rich collection is held by the Canadian Centre for Architecture in Montreal.

Historic photographs

Historic photographs are key tools for architectural and archaeological investigation and aerial survey. They are useful for the study not only of buildings but also of landscapes, industrial archaeology and engineering. This guidance covers sources relating to photography prior to the advent of digital technology: it is necessarily a selective overview. As used here, 'historic' means all images taken prior to the work of living contemporary photographers. Examples here relate to the archives of Historic England, which hold more than 15 million photographs. A guide to this major archive is available as a download from the Historic England Archive website (*see* p 85). Conservation of photographs is a specialist subject: some basic publications and websites are noted on p 84.

Understanding historic photographs is dependent on a complex archival context. Prior to the 1970s, photography in Britain received little consideration or proper recognition and attention remains sporadic. Much photography is apparently only of specialist interest yet it also contains a great deal of 'heritage data' (Fig 4.4). Historic photographs can provide information beyond their apparent 'record' value. An understanding of the apparent subject can be enhanced by knowing who took the image and why. Photographs may reveal an otherwise invisible agenda that can aid interpretation of a site. Original prints and negatives can, in fact, be understood as archaeological artefacts and some at least should be treated as such.

The existence of sufficient annotation, known as metadata, has always been an essential adjunct to any photograph. All photographs depend on an inextricable link between the metadata and the image: for many photographs the metadata has been lost but clues or sources exist which can aid dating, and facilitate the discovery of creators, intentions and new interpretations. Adding new interpretation creates new levels of metadata: if documented, our own subjective reactions to any photograph should be considered as valid as the original intention. Given the anonymity of many images, any later interpretation may actually be the first, so the articulation of new readings should be encouraged. Metadata may be as valuable as the image itself.

Processes

Photographic processes can provide clues to interpretation. Over 1,500 photo-processes are known so the following is a simplified chronological overview. For a detailed discussion of techniques, see the Bibliography on p 84. In addition to the major types discussed below, there are many specialised processes, some of which are unusual outside the short span of years when they were popular. They

Fig 4.4

Although taken as an atmospheric rather than a documentary image, this anonymous photograph including a tide mill and windmill in Walton, Essex, c 1910, is now important because both structures were subsequently demolished. [© Historic England Archive BB80/551]

can be rare even in photographic archives, and expert advice on them should be sought from photographic conservators.

1839–1850s

- **Calotype**
  Invented by William Henry Fox Talbot, this negative–positive process flourished from 1844 to 1851. Fox Talbot travelled extensively and many of his salt prints are associated with fellow estate owners and friends. By the mid-1850s his process was largely superseded by wet collodion (*see below*). Very few architectural views were taken, so any print taken prior to the early 1850s ought to be considered rare. Paper negatives from this era may also survive.

- **Daguerreotype**
  Developed by Louis J M Daguerre from 1839, this was the first viable photographic process and produced a reversed image. Each daguerreotype was extremely vulnerable to damage. Multiple prints or copies are uncommon so many examples are unique. An 1839 view of Whitehall taken by the French photographer St Croix is the first known architectural photograph in the UK. Apart from portraits, daguerreotypes are so rare in the UK that any new examples should become immediate priorities for attention. Even engravings created from daguerreotypes are notably rare.

1852–1860s

- **Wet collodion negatives**
  Introduced in 1851 by Frederick Scott Archer, this process involved glass plates coated with a collodion chemical solution, exposed while still wet. Often with a sepia tone, it became the dominant process alongside thin albumen prints. The sensitivity of the collodion negative only lasted for a short time and the equipment was very unwieldy, thus inhibiting its use in remote locations. Albumen prints remained common up to the 1880s.
- Landscape and architectural photographers continued to use **Calotype** paper negatives and salt prints but they are rarely found after 1860 (these should not be confused with the later Collotype process described below).

1870s–1880s

- **Dry collodion negatives**
  These were developed to avoid the inconveniences of the wet collodion process. Pre-prepared glass plates coated with dry gelatine gave greater emulsion sensitivity. Prints appeared on a range of thicker paper.

- **Carbon, platinum and Woodburytype prints**
  These more expensive processes produced more permanent prints, which are often found bound into contemporary publications.

- **Collotype**
  Mechanical half-tone processes were introduced in this period, but even these could be so expensive that the most sophisticated architectural collotypes are rarely found after the 1920s (although its use continued for postcards and fine art photography).

- *Lantern slides*
  These are glass positives (83 × 102mm) frequently used for lectures from the 1880s up to the 1940s. They are all copies twice-removed from the original negatives and are only significant if the originals do not survive. If taken by amateurs or given hand-colouring they may still be valuable records, but most are duplicates of mass-manufactured commercial views.

1880s

- *Gelatine silver prints*
  Developed from gelatine dry plates, these became the standard print format for many decades. The later development of film (including nitrate film) meant a considerable reduction in equipment weight but these processes were often unsuitable for professional use until the 1940s. *Country Life* and the Royal Commission on the Historical Monuments of England (RCHME) were not unusual in continuing to use glass plates up to 1960.

- *Nitrate and acetate film* were prevalent before 1914 and still in use until the 1990s. They can be easily identified by their distinctive smell. Such film requires separate storage due to its chemical instability – whole collections have been lost due to the fumes from these films affecting stable negatives.

- *Polyester film* began to be introduced, and this stable medium continued in use up to the 1990s.

1908

- *Colour*
  Colour was rare until the 1940s, although Lumiere Autochromes were taken as early as 1908 and the Vivex process was used for portraits as early as 1932. All early colour was very costly. Colour was mostly applied to portraits, gardens, landscapes, stained glass and, very occasionally, interiors. Early 35mm colour stock was expensive and was only available via the USA or Germany, so during the Second World War only well-funded agencies could afford it. Until the 1950s colour was still much more expensive than black and white and images were often produced as large-format transparencies. Colour slides in 35mm form became available around 1955. Due to changes in pigment or fading, early colour views should be considered for digital copying. Colour prints and slides began to disappear in the mid-1990s – like most photographs their value is extremely low if they are not systematically documented.

20th century

- *Traditional processes*
  Until well after the First World War, 'professional' photography still meant the use of large-format glass negatives, which did not disappear until as late as 1960.

- *Digital*
  Digital became prevalent after 1990. In archival terms it is much more problematic than conventional processes, as without the creation of prints the life expectancy and cost of maintaining long-term storage of high-resolution digital files becomes an issue. CDs are thought to have a limited life and the archiving of selected prints is one of the few guarantees of permanency beyond

40 or 50 years. Tagging or embedding information in digital files is absolutely essential: without such measures many architectural and archaeological images will remain visual orphans without any known source or provenance.

Print formats

These are as varied as the processes in which they were used but for albumen prints and later types, print formats became standardised quite quickly in the early 1850s. The standard architectural formats started at 16 × 12 inches and evolved down towards 12 × 10 inches, which lasted until the 1940s. Such prints usually survive only as contacts from similar-sized glass or paper negatives, which seldom survive prior to the 1870s: no negatives at all are known for the first architectural photographer, Roger Fenton (d 1861). Pre-prepared paper negatives of landscapes and architecture survive from between the 1840s and the 1890s. Uniquely, this technique required only lightweight equipment, which facilitated photographing this kind of subject. It is only as late as the 1870s that techniques were developed that allowed for any form of enlargement. Prior to that date, prints could only be created by direct contact printing so negatives were produced according to the print format most in demand.

Dating

Any understanding of the earliest photography in the UK must recognise certain dating conventions – other conventions apply in other countries and even within the UK there are differences between what a researcher might expect to find in England or Scotland; this is often due to licensing restrictions for early processes.

1839 to early 1850s
Before the early 1850s images are so early, so valuable and so vulnerable that it is usually safe to assume all such images have been given a priority in major collections. This may not, however, be the case in minor collections that do not have the resources to identify them or make them available. Despite a huge amount of knowledge about the work of Fox Talbot and Daguerre there is no topographical catalogue of the first photographs of Britain. Any original print or negative taken prior to the early 1860s should be considered as a valuable historical artefact – some will be unique. Many of these exist only in copied form and these later images need adequate metadata for interpretation. Local archives may well contain such early material so curators should be queried concerning their earliest holdings.

1854 to 1864
The formative period in English photography occupies only a few years: most of the earliest records were created during the decade from 1854 to 1864. The Historic England Archive holds hundreds of prints taken during this period, although nothing before 1852. Major photographers are P H Delamotte, Francis Bedford and Roger Fenton (Fig 4.5). As with Fox Talbot's images, a national catalogue of locations represented by these early photographs has yet to be undertaken.

Fig 4.5
Roger Fenton [fl. 1856–1860]
took some of the earliest
topographical photographs of
England. This image, c 1856, of
Whitehall echoes the first ever
photographs of London taken in
1839 by a French photographer.
Because there was no demand for
such photography, such records of
central London are rare: in effect,
the real history of photography
commences in the mid-1850s.
[© Historic England Archive
OP016698]

1860s to 1880s

English photography reached its maturity during the period from the 1860s
to the 1880s, accompanied by the advent of the first professional architectural
photographers. A competitive environment meant that many businesses did not
last long enough to appear in local directories but because they were often taken
over by new businesses, early material can easily exist within apparently later
collections. Competition and the invention of new photographic techniques led
to the lowering of prices. However, for professional architectural photography
costs remained very high and demand was not sufficient to support a specialised
studio, so most photographic activity was linked to portrait work. Heathcote's
directory of every portrait business prior to 1855 (Heathcote and Heathcote
2002) is therefore a useful resource, and the extensive website of the National
Portrait Gallery also contains information on named portrait photographers.
Examples of architectural photographers in this period include Bedford Lemere,
Francis Frith, George Washington Wilson and James Valentine.

By the late 1860s photography had established itself and was also achieving
an image stability which had been vulnerable in preceding years. Less laborious
processes and lower costs made photography less expensive but it was still a
largely professional or rich amateur activity.

An important spur to photography was provided by the invention of the
half-tone: a way of mechanically reproducing photographs. As a consequence,
from the 1880s onwards, architectural journals and magazines began to include
photographic reproductions. Although these are usually inferior to an original
negative or print, some can be of very high quality and even unique; often
the originals can no longer be traced. Postcards using either real or half-tone
photographs vastly multiplied the circulation of images. Despite their ubiquity
some postcards are in fact key records, as they reproduce originals taken before
1900 that no longer survive. An example from the Historic England Archive
collection is a postcard showing the third (now lost) castle at Deal in Kent.

20th century

After the 1890s low costs and cheap cameras brought the first popular photographic period, in which Kodak was a pioneer. At the same time an artistic 'pictorial' movement was prevalent before 1914.

Conventional black and white photographic technologies constantly evolved and viable colour systems became possible by 1908, although they were so expensive that they are rare before the evolution in the mid-1940s of 35mm colour film. Only rich amateurs could afford early colour, which cost three times that of black and white. Private collections of such images may well be discovered in the future.

Digital photography became the norm in the late 1990s. It should be noted that only a tiny proportion of the images taken with 'conventional' photographic processes survives in archives and that an equally small proportion of digital images is expected to survive.

Major architectural and archaeological photographers

Dedicated architectural photography did not exist in England prior to the 1870s. Most professional photographers prior to that date concentrated on portraiture, in which they observed contemporary conventions, used standard processes and were subject to commercial demands. There was no demand for landscapes or architectural images beyond conventional tourist sites, and that market was catered for by the fiercely competitive giant photographic companies such as Francis Frith, J Valentine and George Washington Wilson. Portrait photographers would sometimes take landscapes and architectural subjects on demand, but generally all early architectural and topographical images were taken by amateurs, chemists, antiquaries and photographic clubs. Amateur work proliferated as materials became cheaper and more easily available and it often provides the broadest range of subject matter. Later this mantle was taken over by local photographers, who often made visual surveys of every church and country house, frequently available as postcards.

The first systematic recording of 'threatened buildings' did not take place until the foundation of the Society for Photographing the Relics of London in the 1870s to 1880s. With one or two exceptions the systematic recording of architectural features was never official and such photographic surveys are seldom to be found until after the First World War. Those exceptions are the Royal Commission on the Historical Monuments of England (RCHME), founded in 1908, and the Survey of London, founded in 1894. The visual archives of both of these organisations are now part of the Historic England Archive. For official purposes most photography was contracted out to established architectural photographers like Bedford Lemere.

Bedford Lemere and Company almost single-handedly created the specific subdiscipline of architectural photography in Britain. Operating from the 1870s to the 1940s, Lemere and his son had rivals, but none with such an enduring practice. The other major architectural photographers include S B Bolas, William Ellis of Hackney, Lewis of Birmingham, Edwin Dockree, Charles Latham (linked to *Country Life*), Nathaniel Lloyd, Bill Brandt, Herbert Felton, Eric De Mare, Millar & Harris, and John Gay. All these photographers are represented in the holdings of the Historic England Archive (Fig 4.6).

Fig 4.6

Bill Brandt was commissioned by the National Buildings Record to document churches vulnerable to German bombing. As well as creating a documentary record of Dean Fotherby's monument in Canterbury Cathedral in 1942, he used the opportunity to experiment with lighting and composition. [© Historic England Archive AA42/1330]

Fig 4.7

RAF, Shackleton bomber over Whitehall, *c* 1946. The RAF conducted extensive aerial photography for mapping and training purposes – today such images are reinterpreted quite differently from any original purpose. [© Historic England Archive, B2500]

librarians may be able to provide information about holdings such as the Register of Incorporated Photographers, which later became the Professional Photographers Association. (For the history of professional photographic associations *see* Hannavy 2001.)

Collections of architectural photographs

Collecting historic photographs is a relatively recent practice – even the pioneer collectors only began amassing images in the 1940s, and collectors were still able to create major collections as late as the 1960s and 1970s. The famous American photographic historian Beaumont Newhall, the English antiquary Gerald Cobb (whose archive is at the Historic England Archive) and the collector Helmut Gernsheim (who worked for the National Monuments Record, now incorporated into the Historic England Archive) appear to have been the only people collecting architectural and topographical photographs for most of the 1940s. Early English material is often easier to find outside England: the Gernsheim Collection at the University of Austin, Texas, is one of the most important archives of British photography in the world. Apart from early material in the USA, major English collections are to be found in Scotland, Canada and Australia (*see* pp 84–85). George Washington Wilson and James Valentine were two Scottish photographers of the 1860s. The original archives for both still exist at Aberdeen and St Andrews, respectively (*see* p 85) and contain substantial English material. The archive of the early topographical photographer Russell Sedgefield, born in Wiltshire, includes early views of Stonehenge and is now in Australia.

Sources can be extremely diverse and records of significant heritage value can derive from apparently commercial material. Foreign architectural visitors are known to have taken extensive photographs of England, so collections relating to the UK also exist abroad, especially in the USA. Conversely the domestic oeuvre of English photographers more often associated with work abroad can be poorly defined: William England was a key early photographer for the London Stereoscopic Company but the only known publication on him discusses his work in North America. It is safe to assume that original English material will not only be found in foreign archives but will also be rediscovered in many UK collections.

Photography archives

At least one million historic images are available online as well as substantial biographical data for many thousands of photographers (*see* pp 84–85 for a list of many of these websites). There are also significant and/or substantial photographic holdings of relevance for architecture and archaeology in the Royal Photographic Society collection at the Victoria and Albert Museum; the Hulton Getty Collection; the Canadian Centre for Architecture, Montreal; and the University of Austin, Texas. For photographers after 1915 professional photographic directories should be consulted – many of these are available at the Birmingham Central Library. Websites for private collections are uncommon in the UK but are much more frequent in the USA.

Research questions for historic photographs

Where appropriate, photographic research should be programmed into any recording or survey project from its inception. The default assumption should be that systematic attention has not been applied to architectural, topographical or archaeological subjects. Even within existing specialised archives many architectural and archaeological photographs await discovery and interpretation. If identified they need to be married to new metadata to allow for future retrieval; awareness of the context of the image is vital.

Locating photographs

One of the first tasks is to ascertain the existence of any photographic material for a given locality. Historic photographs can be found in archives, museums, local studies centres, and in private collections. Often basic collections of accumulated images exist in libraries or local history collections but these often only provide undated views without adequate metadata and many derive from later copies; original prints and negatives should always be sought. Ascertaining the degree of coverage for any given site relies on a series of initial questions:

- What catalogued or uncatalogued photographic collections exist for the research subject?

- Who donated these and are there records of the donation?

- What material has been scanned or made available online?

- What publications have surveyed photographic coverage in the research area?

- Are there lists or databases recording the existence of local photographers?

- Are there private collections relating to the area?

- Who has collected local postcards, which are often the primary source?

Once it has been established whether any historic photographs exist for the area under research, there are a number of further questions that should be asked of every image.

What was it taken for?

Nearly all photographs were taken for a specific purpose and what that purpose was is essential to understanding the original image. One should always consider why the site in question was subject to photographic scrutiny.

Events associated with structures, such as destruction or restoration, may have provoked the creation of photographs (Fig 4.8). One of the first conscious photographic surveys was prompted by demolitions; the privately funded Society for Photographing the Relics of Old London produced over 100 early views between 1876 and 1882. Archaeological excavations were also a spur to photographic documentation. Views of digs exist at the Society of Antiquaries, in record offices and in some county archaeological societies; some original prints actually appear in the journals of such societies from the 1860s onwards.

Fig 4.8
W H Mason of Brighton, Chichester Cathedral, 1861. The reconstruction of Chichester Cathedral was aided by documenting the tower's collapse; for the first time photography was used as a surveying tool. Apart from recording such dramatic events there was no perception of any need for the systematic recording of cathedrals – most early images were taken for commercial tourist purposes. [© Historic England Archive CT01/02]

Fig 4.9
Nathaniel Lloyd was an unusual combination of architect and photographer. He systematically documented vernacular structures, such as these oast houses at Great Dixter, East Sussex, c 1925, in order to understand their construction techniques, which he then used to replicate or restore other historic buildings. [© Historic England Archive BB008364]

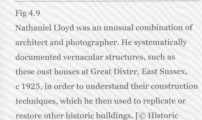

Architects remained loyal to sketches and drawings but from the 1870s onwards they often used photographs as records. Surviving photographic archives of architects are often a mix of informal snaps and professional commissions. Only by the late 1890s was it possible for them to handle cheap and efficient equipment themselves (Fig 4.9). Photography can tie in neatly with architectural drawings: the W D Caröe archive at the Historic England Archive encompasses both measured drawings and many photographs taken or collected by the architect on his travels.

There are types of potential subject that are not represented in the photographic corpus. Obvious themes that are often poorly represented in UK photographic collections include early Victorian industrial structures, commercial or industrial processes, urban domestic architecture (especially interiors and gardens), urban views beyond the tourist trail, the interiors of public houses, suburbs, panoramas from church towers and general views from high vantage points. For the early years of photography (1840s–1870s) many of these gaps are causally linked to identifiable factors:

- Lack of commercial potential: the images would have generated insufficient income to cover costs (although amateurs may have transcended this barrier) (Fig 4.10).

- Absence of patronage: subjects beyond the concerns of large estates or companies failed to attract attention. Tourism is often the main generator of images, but topographical views were dominated by engravings and other nonphotographic media long after photography became viable. Many engravings published from the 1840s onwards actually derive from photographs that are now lost.

- Absence of perceived heritage values: this includes urban, industrial and vernacular structures. Apart from in connection with sites maintained by the Ministry of Works there were no attempts to photograph historic structures systematically and officially until the 1940s.

- Taste: early photographs often adopted a picturesque viewpoint and deliberately omitted industrial or 'modern' subjects as 'vulgar'.

- Lack of institutional links: only large companies and public institutions had the resources to commission photographic records of their own properties, so most photography was driven by private individuals or commercial gain.

- Technical difficulties: interiors were very difficult to execute prior to the 1860s; fading of prints remained a factor even after 1860 and systematic progress in photography only became possible after the 1870s. Few institutions were therefore persuaded that such a problematic form of record was affordable or desirable.

- Costs and rights: daguerreotypes were subject to strict and costly licences in England; all large-format professional photography was very expensive until well after the First World War.

However, there are positive exceptions to these many absences and enquiries should be made for the following types of photography, which may yield unexpected information:

- Stereo photographs: as they were relatively cheap to manufacture, these 'stereocards' often constitute the first known views of locations from 1860 onwards.

- *Carte de visite* photographs: these were also fairly cheap and although they are mostly portraits, a topographical element is often present.

- Photographically illustrated books: before half-tone photographs became possible, real photographs were frequently mounted in books. These often constitute the only known early photograph of a location and may have more value than the book itself. Original mounted photographic prints were superseded by mechanically generated half-tones by the late 1880s: for the latter the original print or negative may still exist.

- Postcards: these became available from the late 1890s and remain the most available early images for many sites. Often they have been poorly copied, so locating original examples may be preferable.

- Collections and publications relating to local photographers, especially those created by the Royal Photographic Society Historical Group.

Fig 4.10
Anon, Monumental Masons in churchyard, stereocard, c 1865. Even though this scene is staged – such stone working would probably have been executed in a studio, not *in situ* – it unusually depicts actual masons. The use of photography to record events was generally motivated by commercial concern, so why this tableau was created is an intriguing question. [© Historic England Archive BB85/3008]

What has been omitted?

Photographs can often deliberately avoid the inclusion of adjoining or nearby structures or features. Early photography mirrored the conventions of landscape painting and deliberately avoided the intrusions of industry and the railway. Any collection that embraces these elements is therefore unusual. Interiors prior to 1860 are equally rare: no interiors of Westminster Abbey, for example, are known prior to this date.

Has the print been manipulated?

The removal or alteration of elements for commercial or artistic purposes was always possible, even before digital photography, but its occurrence was largely determined by the cost of the specialist labour involved. While it could be worthwhile to manipulate commercial or exhibition prints, ordinary photographs of buildings or sites seldom merited such attention. Poor-quality postcards were sometimes manipulated to emphasise outlines.

Is it a copy or an original print?

It is important to note that photographs are often 'surrogates', that is, the version of them that survives is not the actual photographic source, nor does it necessarily reflect the image's original context, which is essential for full interpretation.

The digital era suggests that we are now at the beginning of a period defined by the prevalence of the surrogate. However, the extent of any digitisation is often driven by practical or commercial priorities, so comprehensive digital access cannot be presumed. Historic England has put online more architectural and archaeological material than any commercial photo archive; the fact that even Historic England's photographic web resources represent less than a tenth of its holdings needs to be borne in mind when using other web sources.

Digital records can disappear more quickly and more easily than conventional photographic images. Steps should be taken to preserve both digital images and their metadata by ensuring the archival capture of selected digital images in a form that is known to survive longer than the technology that has generated them. The archival presumption is that the minimum survival span ought to be 50 years. Short-term digital solutions may mean that images fail to survive, so much depends on how photographers and archivists try to ensure longevity.

Research questions for visual sources: a summary

- When was the source made?

- For what purpose was it made?

- Who made it, and for whom?

- What stage of realisation does the source represent?

- What conventions are observed?

- Is the value of the representation heightened or diminished by the skill or knowledge of the originator?

- What technical constraints are imposed by the method or medium employed?

- Does it exist in a number of states? If so, what is the sequence and what is the relationship of each to any actual building or site? Can useful inferences be drawn from variations between the different states?

- Does it form part of a series or set? Do characteristics of the larger group, its scope or its intentions, help in interpreting the individual source?

- What other primary sources, including the building or landscape itself, can shed light on what the source portrays?

- Is there any secondary literature discussing the source? How far can such interpretation be depended upon?

General tips

- Take time getting to know the type of source material being used. The more that is known about how and why it was created, and about its scope and limitations, the more reliably can information be extracted from it.

- Work from original material wherever possible. Reproductions may crop the original, may not allow fine detail or a palimpsest of later annotations to be distinguished, and will not allow you to see if there are helpful inscriptions on the reverse or on any associated wrappers or packaging.

- Make a careful study of the whole of the drawing, map or image, not just the part you are mainly interested in, to ensure that you don't miss valuable clues about date, purpose and provenance.

- Consider the location of the source and its possible relationship to neighbouring or related material. This may help to identify the likely purpose and provenance of the source.

- Compare each source with others to establish its reliability and refine dating. Compare and contrast to identify additions and alterations to the building, setting or wider landscape over time.

- Have regard to existing scholarship relating to the source in hand, but do not accept existing accounts uncritically.

Bibliography

General studies on architectural drawing and design practice

Ackerman, J S 1991 *Distance Points: Essays in Theory and Renaissance Art and Architecture*. Cambridge, MA and London: MIT Press

Ackerman, J S 2002 *Origins, Imitation, Conventions: Representation in the Visual Arts*. Cambridge, MA: MIT Press

Baynes, K and Pugh, H 1981 *The Art of the Engineer*. Guildford: Lutterworth Press

Blau, E and Kaufman, E 1989 *Architecture and its Image: Four Centuries of Architectural Representation*. Montreal and Cambridge, MA: Canadian Centre for Architecture

Booker, P J 1979 *A History of Engineering Drawing*. London and Bury St Edmunds: Northgate

Giddings, B and Horne, M 2002 *Artists' Impressions in Architectural Design*. London: Spon Press

Hambly, M 1988 *Drawing Instruments, 1580–1980*. London: Sotheby

Heawood, E 1950 *Watermarks, Mainly of the 17th and 18th Centuries*. Hilversum: Paper Publications Society

Lever, J (ed) 1963–1986 *Catalogue of the Drawings Collection of the Royal Institute of British Architects*, 20 vols. Farnborough: Gregg

Lever, J 1996 'Architectural drawing' *in* J Turner (ed) *The Dictionary of Art*, **1**, 325–35

Lever, J and Richardson, M 1984 *The Art of the Architect: Treasures from the RIBA's collections*. London: Trefoil

Millon, H A and Lampugnani, V M (eds) 1994 *The Renaissance from Brunelleschi to Michelangelo: The Representation of Architecture*. New York: Rizzoli

Richardson, R and Throne, R 1994 *The Builder Illustrations Index 1843–1883*, London: The Builder Group & Hutton+Rostron in association with The Institute of Historical Research

Taylor, N 1968 *Monuments of Commerce*. Feltham: Country Life Books

Uddin, M S 1997 *Axonometric and Oblique Drawing: A 3-D Construction, Rendering and Design Guide*. New York and London: McGraw-Hill

Architectural drawings and design practice: studies by period

Airs, M 1975 *The Making of the English Country House 1500–1640*. London: Architectural Press

Coldstream, N 1991 *Medieval Craftsmen: Masons and Sculptors*. London: British Museum Press

Dean, D 1983 *The Thirties: Recalling the Architectural Scene*. London: Trefoil

Downes, K 1988 *Sir Christopher Wren: The Design of St Paul's Cathedral*. London: Trefoil

Drexler A 1977 *The Architecture of the Ecole des Beaux-Arts*. London: Secker & Warburg

Geraghty, A 2007 *The Architectural Drawings of Sir Christopher Wren at All Souls College, Oxford: A Complete Catalogue*. Aldershot: Lund Humphries

Gerbino, A and Johnson, S 2009 *Compass and Rule: Architecture as Mathematical Practice in England, 1500–1750*. New Haven, CT and London: Yale University Press

Girouard, M 2009 *Elizabethan Architecture: Its Rise and Fall, 1540–1640*. New Haven, CT and London: Yale University Press

Harris, J 1985 *The Artist and the Country House: A History of Country House and Garden View Painting in Britain 1540–1870*. London: Sotheby's

Harris, J and Higgott, G 1989 *Inigo Jones: Complete Architectural Drawings*. London: Royal Academy of Arts

Laiserin, J 1998 'A brief history of computer aided design'. *Inland Architect*, **115**, 4, 66–74

Lever, J 2003 *Catalogue of the Drawings of George Dance the Younger (1741–1825) and of George Dance the Elder (1695–1768) from the collection of Sir John Soane's Museum*. Oxford: Azimuth Editions

Pinto, J A 1976 'Origins and development of the ichnographic city plan'. *Journal of the Society of Architectural Historians*, **35**, 35–50

Powers, A 2007 *Britain: Modern Architecture in History*. London: Reaktion Books

Richardson, M 1990 'Soane's Use of Drawings'. *Apollo*, **81** (April), 234–41

Snodin, M (ed) 1996 *Sir William Chambers*. London: V&A Publications

Stainton, L and White, C 1987 *Drawing in England from Hilliard to Hogarth*. Cambridge: Cambridge University Press

Stamp, G 1982 *The Great Perspectivists*. London: Trefoil

Tait, A A 1993 *Robert Adam: Drawings and Imagination*. Cambridge: Cambridge University Press

Tait, A A 1996 *Robert Adam: The Creative Mind: From the Sketch to the Finished Drawing*. London: Soane Gallery

Worsley, G 1991 *Architectural Drawings of the Regency Period, 1790–1837, From the Drawings Collection of the Royal Institute of British Architects*. London: Andre Deutsch

Maps

Barber, P and Harper, T 2010 *Magnificent Maps: Power, Propaganda and Art*. London: British Library

Barker, F and Jackson, P 1990 *The History of London in Maps*. London: Barrie & Jenkins

Baynton-Williams, A (ed) 1992 *Town and City Maps of the British Isles 1800–1855*. London: Studio Editions

Bendall, A S 1992 *Maps, Land and Society: A History, with a Carto-Bibliography of Cambridgeshire Estate Maps, c 1600–1836*. Cambridge: Cambridge University Press

Bendall, A S (ed) 1997 (2nd edn) *The Dictionary of Land Surveyors and Local Mapmakers of Great Britain and Ireland 1530–1850*, 2 vols. London: British Library

Black, J 1997 *Maps and History: Constructing Images of the Past*. New Haven and London: Yale University Press

Chibnall, J 1995 (3rd edn) *A Directory of UK Map Collections*. Cambridge: British Cartographic Society on behalf of the Map Curators' Group

Delano-Smith, C and Kain, R J P 1999 *English Maps: A History*. London: British Library

Foot, W 1994 *Maps for Family History: A Guide to the Records of the Tithe, Valuation Office, and National Farm Surveys of England and Wales, 1836–1943*, PRO Readers' Guide 9

Foxell, S 2007 *Mapping London: Making Sense of the City*. London: Black Dog

Foxell, S 2008 *Mapping England*. London: Black Dog

Glanville, P 1972 *London in Maps*. London: The Connoisseur

Harvey, P D A 1993 *Maps in Tudor England*. Chicago: The University of Chicago Press

HMSO 1967 *Maps and Plans in the Public Record Office: 1 British Isles, c 1410–1860*. London: HMSO

Kain, R J P (ed) 2008 *An Atlas and Index of the Tithe Files of Mid-19th Century England and Wales*. Cambridge: Cambridge University Press

Kain, R J P and Prince, H C 1985 *The Tithe Surveys of England and Wales*. Cambridge: Cambridge University Press

Kain, R J P and Prince, H C 2000 *Tithe Surveys for Historians*. Chichester: Phillimore

Kain, R J P and Prince, H C 2015 *British Town Maps: A History*. London: British Library

Nicolson, N and Hawkyard, A (eds) 1988 *The Counties of Britain: A Tudor Atlas by John Speed*. London: Pavilion

Oliver, R 1993 (3rd edn, 2013) *Ordnance Survey Maps: A Concise Guide for Historians*. London: Charles Close Society

Oliver, R 2014 *The Ordnance Survey in the 19th Century: Maps, Money and the Growth of Government*. London: Charles Close Society

Ordnance Survey of Great Britain (1991) *England and Wales. Indexes to the 1/2500 and 6-inch Scale Maps*. Southampton: OS, c 1905–6; rpt, with an introduction by R Oliver

Saxton, C 1992 *Christopher Saxton's 16th Century Maps: The Counties of England & Wales*, with an introduction by W Ravenhill. Shrewsbury: Chatsworth Library

Schofield, J (ed) 1987 *The London Surveys of Ralph Treswell*. London: Topographical Society

Seymour, W A (ed) 1980 *A History of the Ordnance Survey*. Folkestone: Dawson

Models

Briggs, M 1929 'Architectural Models-I'. *The Burlington Magazine for Connoisseurs*, **54**, 313, 174–75, 178–81 and 183

Briggs, M 1929 'Architectural Models-II'. *The Burlington Magazine for Connoisseurs*, **54**, 314, 245–47 and 250–52

Moon, K 2003 *Modelling Messages. The Architect and the Model*. New York: Monacelli Press

Morris, M 2006 *Models: Architecture and the Miniature*. London: John Wiley

Smith, A C 2004 *Architectural Model as Machine: A New View of Models from Antiquity to the Present Day*. Oxford and Burlington: Architectural Press

Physick, J and Darby, M 1973 *Marble Halls: Drawings and Models for Victorian Secular Buildings*. London: V&A

Wilton-Ely, J 1967 'The Architectural Model'. *Architectural Review*, **142** (July), 27–32

Topography

Barley, M W 1974 *A Guide to British Topographical Collections*. London: Council for British Archaeology

Bonehill, J and Daniels, S (eds) 2009 *Paul Sandby: Picturing Britain, A Bicentenary Exhibition*. London: Royal Academy of Arts

Clayton, T 1997 *The English Print 1688–1802*. New Haven, CT and London: Yale University Press

Gascoigne, B 2004 (2nd edn) *How to Identify Prints: A Complete Guide to Manual and Mechanical Processes from Woodcut to Inkjet*. London: Thames & Hudson

Hunter, M (ed) 2010 *Printed Images in Early Modern Britain: Essays in Interpretation*. Farnham: Ashgate

Payne, A 1987 *Views of the Past: Topographical Drawings in the British Library*. London and Wolfeboro, NH: The Library

Russell, R 1979 *Guide to British Topographical Prints*. Newton Abbot: David & Charles

Additional visual sources

Alcock, N W 1986 (2nd edn, 2001) *Old Title Deeds: A Guide for Local and Family Historians*. Chichester: Phillimore

Gaskell, S M 1983 *Building Control: National Legislation and the Introduction of Local Bye-Laws in Victorian England*. London: Bedford Square Press

Hollowell, S 2000 *Enclosure Records for Historians*. Chichester: Phillimore

Hudson, G 2008 *The Design and Printing of Ephemera in Britain and America 1720–1920*. London: British Library/Oak Knoll Press

Menuge, A (ed) 2016 *Understanding Historic Buildings: A Guide to Good Recording Practice*. Swindon: Historic England

Porter, S 1990 *Exploring Urban History: Sources for Local Historians*. London: Batsford

RCAHMS 2004 *Creating a Future for the Past: The Scottish Architects' Papers Preservation Project*. Edinburgh: RCAHMS

Rowley, G 1984 *British Fire Insurance Plans*. Old Hatfield: Chas E Goad

Thom, C 2005 *Researching London's Houses: An Archives Guide*. Whitstable: Historical Publications

Photography

Baldwin, G et al 2004 *All the Mighty World*. New York: Yale University Press

Barber, M 2011 *A History of Aerial Photography and Archaeology*. Swindon: English Heritage

Cole, S 2017 *Photographing Historic Buildings*. Swindon: Historic England

Cooper, N 1976 *The Opulent Eye: Late Victorian and Edwardian Taste in Interior Design*. London: The Architectural Press

Cooper, N 2011 *The Photography of Bedford Lemere & Co.* Swindon: English Heritage

Crawford, A 1982 'In praise of collotype: architectural illustration at the turn of the century'. *Architectural History*, **25**, 56–64

Elwall, R 1994 *Photography Takes Command: The Camera and British Architecture, 1890–1939*. London: RIBA Heinz Gallery

Gernsheim, H 1969 (rev edn) *The History of Photography: From the Camera Obscura to the Beginning of the Modern Era*. London: Thames and Hudson

Gernsheim, H 1984 *Incunabula of British Photographic Literature: A Bibliography of British Photographic Literature, 1839–75, and British Books Illustrated with Original Photographs*. London and Berkeley: Scolar Press

Hannavy, J 2001 *Images of a Century: Celebrating the Centenary of the British Institute of Professional Photography 1901–2001*. Ware: British Institute of Professional Photography

Hannavy, J (ed) 2008 *Encyclopedia of 19th Century Photography*. New York/London: Routledge

Harker, M 1979 *The Linked Ring: The Secession Movement in Photography in Britain, 1892–1910*. London: Heinemann

Heathcote, B and Heathcote, P 2002 *A Faithful Likeness: The First Photographic Portrait Studios in the British Isles 1841–1855*. Lowdham: Bernard & Pauline Heathcote

Leith, I 2001 'Amateurs, antiquaries and tradesmen: a context for photographic history in London'. *London Topographical Society*, **28**, 91–118

Leith, I 2005 *Delamotte's Crystal Palace: A Victorian Pleasure Dome Revealed*. Swindon: English Heritage

Samuel, R 1996 *Theatres of Memory: Past and Present in Contemporary Culture*. London: Verso

Saunders, A 2008 *Historic Views of London: Photographs from the Collection of B E C Howarth-Loomes*. Swindon: English Heritage

Seaborne, M 1995 *Photographers' London 1839–1994*. London: Museum of London

Stamp, G 1984 *The Changing Metropolis: Earliest Photographs of London 1839–1879*. Harmondsworth: Viking

Taylor, R 2007 *Impressed by Light: British Photographers from Paper Negatives, 1840–1860*. New York: Yale University Press

Thomas, C 1988 *Views and Likenesses: Early Photographers and their Work in Cornwall and the Isles of Scilly, 1839–1870*. Truro: Royal Institution of Cornwall

Turley, R V 2001 *Isle of Wight Photographers 1840–1940*. Southampton: University of Southampton Libraries

Photographic processes and conservation

Baldwin, G 1991 *Looking at Photographs: A Guide to Technical Terms*. Malibu, CA: J Paul Getty Museum

Benson, R 2008 *The Printed Picture*. New York: Museum of Modern Art

Coe, B and Haworth-Booth, M 1983 *A Guide to Early Photographic Processes*. Westerham: Hurtwood

Lavedrine, B 2009 *Photographs of the Past: Process and Preservation*. Los Angeles: Getty Conservation Institute

Nadeau, L 1994 *Encyclopedia of Printing, Photographic and Photomechanical Processes*. New Brunswick: Atelier Luis Nadeau

Reilly, J R 1986 *Care and Identification of 19th-Century Photographic Prints*. Rochester, NY: Eastman Kodak

Online resources

Aerofilms (aerial coverage of Britain from 1919): www.britainfromabove.org.uk

Artists' Papers Register (a register of the archives of artists and craftspeople which includes many architects): www.apr.ac.uk/artists/home.htm

The British Library: http://imagesonline.bl.uk and its database of 19th-century periodicals like the *Penny Illustrated Paper*, published 1861–1913 at: www.bl.uk/onlinegallery/index.html

British Library (Photographic Processes): www.bl.uk/onlinegallery/features/photographicproject/photographicprocesses.html

British Library (Photographically Illustrated Books): www.bl.uk/catalogues/photographyinbooks/welcome.htm

British Newspaper Archive: www.britishnewspaperarchive.co.uk/

The British Museum: www.britishmuseum.org/research/collection_online/search.aspx

Catalogue of British Town Maps: http://townmaps.data.history.ac.uk

Charles Booth poverty maps (from 1887; at London School of Economics): http://booth.lse.ac.uk

City of London Collections (includes the Civic Survey of Greater London, 1917): http://collage.cityoflondon.gov.uk

Country Life (archive of photographs mainly of country house from c 1900 onwards): www.countrylifeimages.co.uk

Courtauld Institute of Art: www.artandarchitecture.org.uk

The Crown Estate (McInnes, R and Stubbings, H *A coastal historical resources guide for England*): www.thecrownestate.co.uk

Digital Historic Map Archive (low-resolution images of maps to order): www.old-maps.co.uk/maps.html

Directory of Photograph Collections in the UK: www.directoryphotographiccollectionsuk.org/pub/apps/resources

Edinburgh photographers (like many non-English sources this website contains substantial English content): www.edinphoto.org.uk

Francis Frith online catalogue (for the Francis Frith negative archive contact the Birmingham Reference Library. Note that Frith took over the negatives of earlier architectural photographers such as P H Delamotte and R Fenton which then were merged within this large company – some of these are actually online but the original photographer is unidentified). This website also displays a selection of historic maps: www.francisfrith.com

George Eastman House archive: https://eastman.org/collections-online

George Washington Wilson archive at the University of Aberdeen (contains extensive English topographical views): www.abdn.ac.uk/special-collections/george-washington-wilson.php

Guildhall Library and London Metropolitan Archives, Corporation of London (over 20,000 images of London available online): http://collage.cityoflondon.gov.uk

Historic England Archive: http://archive.historicengland.org.uk provides a portal to all other HE websites and scanned holdings. For a selective guide to the contents of the HE Archive (in 2018) a download is available at http://archive.historicengland.org.uk/Catalogues/Default.aspx

Historic Maps: www.mapco.net

Illustrated London News (views of London from 1842 to present): www.iln.org.uk

Incorporated Church Building Society (1818 to 1982; thousands of plans and drawings from 15,000 files relating to applications by parishes for grants from the Society; originals now deposited in Lambeth Palace Library, but detached group of 700 drawings, 1818–54, at the Society of Antiquaries): www.lambethpalacelibrary.org/contents/icbs

James Valentine archive at St Andrews University Library (contains extensive English topographical views): www.st-andrews.ac.uk/library/specialcollections/collections/archives/themanuscriptcollections/businessrecords/valentine

Landmark Historical Map Pack (registration needed): www.landmark.co.uk/

Library of Congress Photographic Home Page: www.loc.gov/pictures/

London photographers (an A–Z of photographers active from 1839 to 1900): www.photolondon.org.uk

Mary Evans Picture Library (a general picture library which includes the Illustrated London News archive): www.maryevans.com

Motco (selection of early London maps, also available on CD): www.motco.com/

Museum of London (over 35,000 images of London and its people): www.museumoflondonimages.com

National Archives (see also the National Register of Archives for information on the nature and location of manuscripts and historical records that relate to British History, and Access to Archives, also known as A2A, a database of archives held in local record offices in England and Wales, now part of the Discovery collection): www.nationalarchives.gov.uk www.nationalarchives.gov.uk/nra/default.asp

The National Art Library: www.vam.ac.uk/content/articles/n/national-art-library-catalogue

National Library of Scotland: https://maps.nls.uk/

Old Maps Online: https://www.oldmapsonline.org

Ordnance Survey (commercial website for purchasing modern-day and facsimile historic maps; general advice on sources): www.ordnancesurvey.co.uk

Ordnance Survey historic 6-inch maps: http://maps.nls.uk/os/6inch-england-and-wales

Photographic conservation issues are discussed at http://graphicatlas.org and http://www.smp-photoconservation.com

Photographic Exhibitions in Britain (excellent provenance for many key photographers from 1839 to 1865): http://peib.dmu.ac.uk

Research Historic Buildings in the British Isles (general website with many useful links): www.buildinghistory.org

Royal Institute of British Architects (RIBA) Library: The RIBA's online catalogue allows you to search 300 main architectural periodicals, books and audio-visual material in the library, the holdings of the RIBA Library Photographs Collection, drawings, manuscripts and archives in the RIBA Library Drawings and Archives Collection, and a biographical database of architects. The RIBA photograph collection includes an archive from the Architectural Press, publishers of the Architects' Journal and the Architectural Review: http://riba.sirsidynix.net.uk/uhtbin/webcat (for written material, archives and drawings) http://architecture.com/image-library (for photographs, or simply search 'RIBApix')

Royal Photographic Society Historical Group: a series of publications on photographers deriving from directories of UK cities & counties. Details at http://www.rps.org/group/Historical

Royal Photographic Society Exhibitions, 1870–1915 (excellent provenance for many amateur and pictorial photographers): http://erps.dmu.ac.uk

Sir John Soane's Museum. A concise catalogue lists all 30,000 architectural drawings at www.soane.org/drawings. Parts of the collection (including English baroque drawings and many from the office of Sir John Soane) are catalogued online: http://www.soane.org/signposts/search-collection

Society of Antiquaries of London (a database of over 4,100 entries on drawings and other items): http://archaeologydataservice.ac.uk/archives/view/SoA_images

Victoria and Albert Museum (V&A): http://collections.vam.ac.uk

William Henry Fox Talbot (complete online correspondence: check for named sites and landowners): www.foxtalbot.dmu.ac.uk

William Henry Fox Talbot Catalogue Raisonné. This resource from the Bodleian Library provides access to the complete corpus of Fox Talbot's work on paper, and a catalogue browseable by themes: www.foxtalbot.bodleian.ox.ac.uk

Index